Information rights for records managers

Information rights for records managers

Rachael Maguire

facet publishing

Published by Facet Publishing,
7 Ridgmount Street, London WC1E 7AE
www.facetpublishing.co.uk

Facet Publishing is wholly owned by CILIP: the Library and Information Association.

British Library Cataloguing in Publication Data
A catalogue record for this book is available from the British Library.

ISBN 978-1-78330-244-4 (paperback)
ISBN 978-1-78330-245-1 (hardback)
ISBN 978-1-78330-246-8 (e-book)

First published 2019

Text printed on FSC accredited material.

MIX
Paper from responsible sources
FSC® C013604

Typeset from author's files in 11/14pt Palatino and OpenSans by Flagholme Publishing Services
Printed and made in Great Britain by CPI Group (UK) Ltd, Croydon, CR0 4YY.

To Gary and William

Contents

Acknowledgements

Thanks to my husband, Gary, for all the proofreading and to my godmother, Carolynn Larson, for reviewing and making suggestions. Thanks to Dr Jane Secker for talking me through the process at the start. Finally, thanks to Kevin Haynes, my manager at London School of Economics, for providing support in writing this book.

Rachael Maguire

1

Introduction to information rights law

Introduction

There are very few people working in information rights law who intended to do so. Most people managing requests for information under data protection or freedom of information started in another discipline like records management, information management, archives or as librarians and then transferred over or had information rights added to their duties. Some of the principles are the same. Records management and data protection both require that data is destroyed when it is no longer required. Librarians and archivists are used to helping people to find the information they need from within their collections. I came myself from a records management background.

However, the various pieces of legislation covering information rights have specific legal requirements relating to the information that an organization holds. If you find yourself managing information rights requests you need to be aware of what is in the legislation. There are courses, including master's degrees, available in this area. For example, I received the LLM Information Rights Law at University of Northumbria. However, not everyone has the time or funds to study at that level, but you still need to know how to apply the law.

That's what this book is for. It is intended to help records managers, information managers, archivists and librarians who find themselves with responsibility for managing information rights in their organizations. As such, it goes through the big three – Data Protection,

Freedom of Information and the Environmental Information Regulations – as well as the other legislation in this area that covers how you should respond to requests for information. Not all of this will apply to everyone; for example, access to health records is unlikely to be used by organizations that do not hold health records, but the Privacy and Electronic Communications Regulations apply wherever marketing takes place. If you are acting as your organization's expert in this area, this book will point to most if not all of the legislation that you need to know about, going into detail about the UK-based legislation in this area.

The focus of the book is on UK-based legislation. This includes the specific Scottish legislation relating to freedom of information and environmental information. However, the data protection advice is based on the General Data Protection Regulation (GDPR). This applies Europe wide, so it will be useful to anyone working with data protection in the European Union (EU). You will have to be mindful of your local legislation, as the derogations in the GDPR mean that national governments can choose certain elements for themselves, for example, whether to consider that children can consent at age 13 or 16. If you are outside the EU but processing the personal data of EU citizens, you are technically covered by the GDPR as well, so it is worth knowing what it covers. The source of the environmental information regulations is an international treaty, the Aarhus Convention, that most European countries have signed up to. While they will have their own regulations, it is likely that the discussion on what environmental information is will still apply. And while the details of freedom of information may differ in each Act, the method of managing requests is still likely to be useful, whichever legal regime you are under.

This chapter gives a brief overview of what information rights law is and what it covers from a UK perspective, including the legislation specific to Scotland. This includes information on the regulators for these laws. If you are looking for more specific information, you should refer to the individual chapters of the book:

Chapter 2: Freedom of information: based on the UK and Scottish Acts, how to recognise a request and to how to draft a response.

Chapter 3: Freedom of information exemptions: how to apply the exemptions, dealing with requests for internal review and complaints to the Information Commissioner's Office and beyond.

Chapter 4: Data Protection Act to General Data Protection Regulation (GDPR): the evolution from managing personal data under the old UK Data Protection Act to the new requirements of the GDPR and new UK Data Protection Act.

Chapter 5: Data protection requests: managing requests for and relating to personal data from data subjects.

Chapter 6: Data protection enquiries: the likely enquiries you will get from staff relating to data protection, including privacy notices and data protection impact assessments.

Chapter 7: Environmental Information Regulations: based on the UK and Scottish Regulations, how to recognise and respond to requests for environmental information.

Chapter 8: Other information rights laws: based on the UK, covers access to medical records, the Privacy and Electronic Communications Regulations and other legislation that you need to be aware of, depending on what your organization does.

Chapter 9: Records management: the basic methods of managing records so that you can easily respond to information rights requests.

Chapter 10: Resources: links to the resources available online to help you with your information rights work.

What is information rights law?

Information rights is a term covering legislation that allows you to request information from a public sector organization. However, private organizations are also covered for personal data and some information that they provide to public sector organizations, either through the work they do for those organizations or due to regulatory purposes. Information rights started with the Swedish Freedom of Information Act more than 200 years ago, but have expanded to cover personal and environmental information, with specific legislation for different types of information introduced where required.

The three main pieces of legislation cover requests for:

- general information – usually via a freedom of information or access to information act;

- personal information – in Europe, this will be via data protection legislation, which covers how personal data is treated as well as allowing individuals to request their own data. Other parts of the world may have privacy acts that cover one or both of these aspects of data protection;
- environmental information – in Europe, this will be under environmental information regulations or similar legislation.

In the United Kingdom the respective items of legislation are: the Freedom of Information Act 2000/Freedom of Information (Scotland) Act 2002; the Data Protection Act 1998 up to late May 2018 and the General Data Protection Regulation/new Data Protection Act 2018 thereafter; and the Environmental Information Regulations 2004/Environmental Information (Scotland) Regulations 2004.

What else is available?

The above provide the main access rights but there is also legislation specifically covering access to:

- medical records, directly from medical professionals
- local government records, for example, council minutes and accounts.

There are also related acts, regulations and codes of practice that determine what public bodies themselves or third parties can do with information produced by public bodies:

- Re-use of Public Sector Information Regulations 2005. These allow third parties to use public sector information for publication and other commercial purposes. They come from an EU Directive.
- Privacy and Electronic Communications Regulations 2015. These cover marketing, particularly electronic forms of marketing. They come from an EU Directive.
- Computer Misuse Act 1990. This Act deals with information security issues. The UK Act came first, and has been used as a model by Canada and New Zealand.
- Public Records Act 1958. There have been several Acts relating to

management of records, at first to ensure that the right records went to state archives. The UK and Scottish Freedom of Information Acts also require a code of practice on managing records, so as to ensure that the requirements relating to the provision of information can be properly carried out.
- INSPIRE Regulations 2009. These cover the transfer of spatial datasets between public authorities, and relate to the Environmental Information Regulations.

This legislation will be covered in Chapter 8.

Who works in information rights law?

Information rights law is a fairly recent field. As stated above, very few people come into it directly through a training course or degree. Due to its close relationship with information management (you cannot provide the requested information if you are not managing it) a lot of people who end up in the information rights field have come from a records management, library or general information management background. We know the principles of managing information and extend these principles to providing the information on request. As will be discussed in Chapter 9, a good records management programme helps to provide the information requested, partially by making sure that it is available and partially by making sure that it is the right information.

However, the 'law' part of information rights law is important. While the Information Commissioners' (UK and Scottish) guidance is good to follow and useful, a knowledge of how to approach the law itself will make handling the responsibilities created by the law much more effective. For example, reading the guidance on section 40 of the Freedom of Information Act 2000 will help you to determine what personal data you can exempt from release. Reading section 40 in the Act itself will help you to determine if you are applying section 40(3), if release would breach the data protection principles or section 40(4), or if the information would be exempt from release to the data subject so cannot be released to anyone else. This will be important if you get a complaint about a response lodged with the regulator, as they will be arguing from the relevant section of the Act and will expect the same from you.

While you have to balance the readability of a response with acknowledging the law, the ability to cite the correct subsections of the legislation will help, if you think that a complaint may be made to the Information Commissioner's Office/Scottish Information Commissioner or to the courts. The intention of this book is to help you to engage better with the legislation so as to sharpen your responses to requests for information.

General access to information

Freedom of information, also known as access to information, is the right to ask for information from public bodies. The first Freedom of Information Act was enacted in Sweden in 1766. Finland and the United States followed in the mid-20th century, with Australia, New Zealand and Canada producing their Acts in the early 1980s. Since the start of the 1990s, many more countries around the world have enacted freedom of information, bringing the total at the end of 2016 to 115 countries.[1] Federated countries like the United States, Germany and Australia also have specific acts for their constituent states. Some countries include a right to information or documents in their constitution, while others have specific legislation. Some countries or states require payment of a fee, while others allow free access to information, although there may be a limit as to how much work a public body must carry out to provide the information – as, for example, the cost limit in the UK and Scottish Acts. A fee may be payable for any disbursements such as for photocopying.

The focus of all this legislation is on access to information held by and generated by the public sector. Exemptions to release are usually available and will normally cover:

- national security and defence
- commercial-in-confidence information
- third-party personal information
- confidential information
- information relating to law enforcement and the courts.

However, the exemptions in particular Acts can vary in different countries. For example, the US Federal Freedom of Information Act exempts 'geographical information relating to wells'.[2] The Australian Federal Freedom of Information Act exempts information that could damage Commonwealth relations. Finland's exemptions include the results of or information about psychological testing.

Private sector bodies are usually not directly covered by the legislation. However, private sector information will be available under freedom of information, due to its being collected and held by public bodies. This is the main reason for the commercial confidentiality clauses in the UK and Scottish Freedom of Information Acts (see Chapter 3 on section 43, commercial-in-confidence information, page 64). Some self-supporting public bodies may also want to use these exemptions. Private companies which are wholly owned by public sector organizations will be covered. Others are covered by legislation on access to environmental information, due to having public duties or duties of a public nature, e.g. health professionals in Estonia.

In the UK generally, the Information Commissioner's Office (ICO) regulates the UK Freedom of Information Act (FoIA). In Scotland, the Scottish Information Commissioner (SIC) regulates the Freedom of Information (Scotland) Act (FoISA). This means that they deal with any complaints about the way a request has been handled and can provide notices relating to the management of freedom of information (FoI) requests and records management to poorly performing organizations. Requesters or public sector organizations not happy with an ICO or SIC decision can appeal further through the court system of their respective country.

Access to personal information

In Europe, access to and proper management of personal data was covered by the Directive 95/46/EC on the protection of individuals with regard to the processing of personal data and on the free movement of such data until 24 May 2018. After that date the Directive was replaced by the General Data Protection Regulation (GDPR) and Directive 2016/680 'on the protection of natural persons with regard to the processing of personal data by competent authorities for the purposes of the prevention, investigation, detection or prosecution of criminal offences or the execution of criminal penalties, and on the free movement of such data' (Crime Directive). The UK government has created a new Data Protection Act (DPA) which combines both the GDPR and the Crime Directive. Other countries may include access to personal information within general access to information laws or have privacy laws which cover some of the same territory as data protection law. Countries with similar laws to the Directive 95/46/EC are recognised as such by the EU, which is useful for European Economic Area (EEA)[3] countries that want to share personal data with them.

The origins of the original Directive on personal data are in the 1980s and the human right to privacy. The early focus was on personal information stored on and processed by computers, although the later Directive widened this to paper files which easily identify the individual concerned.

Data protection has its own terminology. Organizations which control the processing of personal data are known as data controllers. Third parties which process personal data on a data controller's behalf are known as data processors. Individuals whose personal data are being processed are known as data subjects. The notices on forms and websites that tell you what will be done with your data are known as privacy notices.

Within the data protection regime, requests for your own information are known as 'subject access requests'. The Durant judgment limited a subject access request to firstly

> whether the information is biographical in a significant sense, that is, going beyond the recording of the putative data subject's involvement in a matter or an event that has no personal connotations, a life event in respect of which his privacy could not be said to be compromised. The second is one of focus. The information should have the putative data subject as its focus rather than some other person with whom he may have been involved or some transaction or event in which he may have figured or have had an interest.[4]

From the same paragraph, the judge in the case, Auld, ruled that 'Mere mention of a data subject in a document' did not constitute personal data. While the concept of the information needing to be about the person was generally used to focus a subject access request, it has been found in other circumstances that a person's name can constitute personal data in and of itself.[5] The GDPR widens the definition of what constitutes personal data, so a name is considered personal data in and of itself and all documents mentioning the name should be provided. In practice, it is sometimes easier to provide all material where an individual is mentioned, just to be thorough.

Data protection is unusual in information rights as it covers more than just requests for information. It covers the processing of personal data more generally, no matter whether this processing is carried out by public or private sector organizations and includes keeping to the data protection principles (see Chapter 3).[6] Specific requirements of the previous UK DPA include:

- requests to stop processing information, particularly in relation to marketing;
- requests to change inaccurate information;
- a requirement on organizations to identify a reason for processing the personal data, known as a condition for processing. In the UK, these are based on those listed in Schedules 2 and 3 of the DPA and include consent and legitimate interests of the data controller amongst other things;
- registering as a data controller with the Information Commissioner, which includes providing a list of the types of personal data you will collect from, whom, and whom you will share it with;
- ensuring that when you are collecting personal information you inform individuals why you need the data and what you will use it for;
- setting out a separate list of sensitive personal data, including health and criminal offences, which require specific conditions for processing, including explicit consent;
- determining how data should be transferred between countries in the EEA and worldwide;
- setting out exemptions to both providing data via subject access requests and informing an individual if their data is being processed.

The GDPR expands on some of these requirements and introduces some new rights such as the right of portability and requirements such as record keeping. Post Brexit, the UK's new DPA will need to meet its requirements in order to allow the processing of the personal data of EU citizens.

Data Protection interacts with FoI in the UK through specific exemptions in the FoIA and FoISA.[7] In both exemptions, subject access requests are meant to be dealt with via the DPA. Requests for third-party personal information need to be considered in line with the data protection principles and exemptions in the DPA.

As the DPA covers the whole of the UK, including Scotland, the regulator is the ICO, although obviously the SIC has to consider the DPA when considering the personal data exemption in the FoISA. The ICO can set fines for security breaches and other non-compliance with the DPA. Fines for other non-compliance can be set higher now that the GDPR has come into force.

Access to environmental information

Access to environmental information as a specific class of information in Europe and Central Asia comes from the UN Economic Commission for Europe agency (UNECE) Convention on Access to Information, Public Participation in Decision-making and Access to Justice in Environmental Matters, usually known as the Aarhus Convention, which was held in 1998. An EU Directive followed (Directive 2003/4/EC of the European Parliament and of the Council of 28 January 2003 on public access to environmental information and repealing Council Directive 90/313/EEC), through which it was intended that EU members would create their own legislation. In the UK, this is the Environmental Information Regulations 2005 (EIR). Scotland has its own regulations, although these are fairly similar. Access to environmental information is one of the three pillars of the Aarhus Convention, which is also intended to promote public participation and help the public to gain justice in environmental matters.

The USA has an earlier Act, the Emergency Planning and Community Right-to-Know Act (EPCRA), which was passed in 1986 with the purpose of informing people about any chemical accidents that occur within their communities. As such, this Act has a narrower purpose than the EIR, being somewhat tied in with occupational health and safety law. Both Australia and Canada have followed the US model, rather than the EU one.

In spite of the intention to make environmental information available to the general public, in my experience, knowledge of the EIR is fairly low. It is rare that a requester will specify that they are making a request under the Regulations; most mention FoI if they reference a law at all. If you are covered by the Regulations, you will need to be aware of the definition of environmental information so that you know which set of exemptions to apply and do not get caught out trying to apply an FoI exemption where you should use the EIR exception instead.

The EIR define fairly exhaustively what environmental information is, but leave some room for interpretation. Chapter 7 goes into the definition in detail, and also covers information relating to land, land use, waterways, emissions into the environment and the built environment. There are several similarities to the FoI Acts; for example, a 20-day response time. However, there are also differences, such as being able to make verbal as well as written requests. Like FoI, the focus is on providing the information, with the other two pillars of the Aarhus Convention supported by the access rights made available in the Regulations.

There is more scope for private bodies to be covered by the EIR than by the FoI Acts. It was recognised at the Convention and the Directive stages that some countries have public utilities, and so would be completely covered by the Regulations. However, other countries have privatised utilities that hold the same type of information but which could be rendered unavailable. The compromise was to include within the Regulations private utilities and other bodies that still have some public duties. As such, water companies in the UK are partially covered by the EIR because they have public duties relating to the environment that, for example, give them special powers for access to land. Public bodies with environmental duties will need to check to see if they are covered by the EIR, even if they are definitely not covered by FoI.

Both the UK FoIA and the FoISA contain exemptions for environmental information that point to the EIR. The decision to have two separate pieces of legislation was due to the restrictive nature of the exceptions offered in Directive 2003/4/EC, which did not give scope for the range, nor the absolute exemptions, now contained in the UK FoIA.

Like the FoI Acts, the EIR have an exception relating to personal data, which points to the DPA for subject access requests and applies similar tests for third-party personal data.

Unlike the FoI Acts, the EIR do allow for the exception of information, due to intellectual property rights. However, this is a difficult exception to apply.

The ICO regulates the UK EIR, while the SIC regulates the Scottish EIR. Both will require organizations to have used the relevant legislation – EIR as opposed to FoI – and will require that organizations make the relevant arguments for exceptions if the information requested is judged to be environmental in nature.

Conclusion

Generally, the legislation in this area governs how an organization should handle a request for information. The following chapters take you through what that means in practice. The three main areas of legislation – FoI, data protection and environmental information – have developed at different times but all require being open about the information you are creating. FoI specifically requires public authorities to be clear how tax money is being spent and how they are treating citizens. Data protection requires all organizations managing personal data to be transparent about what they are doing with that data. The EIR extends FoI into non-public authorities that still have an environmental effect on the general public.

Data protection extends as to how you should manage the personal data it covers, though it could be said that the codes of practice for records management in both the FoIA and FoISA determine how public sector organizations manage their information as well. The Article 30 requirements to record processing activities are the best booster for records management that we have had for a long time as they do not just cover the public sector.

As such, this book covers recognising a request and includes some pointers towards using the legislation to help bolster your records management programme. As I have said about the GDPR, I finally have a legal requirement to manage records, and nobody can stop me!

2

Freedom of information

Introduction

This is the first of two chapters on how to respond to a request for information made under the UK and Scottish Freedom of Information (FoI) Acts. The UK Freedom of Information Act (FoIA) covers English, Welsh and Northern Irish public authorities and any public authorities which operate across the UK. The Freedom of Information (Scotland) Act (FoISA) covers Scottish public authorities only. While similar to the FoIA, the FoISA does deviate from it, particularly in the matter of exemptions.

Covered in this chapter are:

- the basic method for handling a request, which is also useful for the EIR;
- how to recognise a request;
- how to process a request;
- how to handle requests for clarification;
- how to create a response.

Covered in Chapter 3 are:

- the exemptions and how to apply them;
- dealing with internal reviews;
- dealing with complaints to the Information Commissioner's Office

(ICO) and Scottish Information Commissioner (SIC));
- managing the publication scheme.

In both chapters, when I refer to 'you' I am thinking of the records manager or information manager who finds themselves in the position of having to manage responses to FoI requests. You can read through the whole of both chapters or dip into the parts that have the most relevance for you. I suggest reading through all of this chapter if you are completely new to FoI, as it covers not just how to process a request but also how to recognise a request or a non-request, and how to deal with vexatious and repeated requests. Most requests that you deal with will be to find information, package it and send it out, but others will be more tricky and this chapter provides guidance on how to process those trickier requests.

Handling requests: the basic method

The basic method for a one-person or small team to deal with a request for information is set out below. All points are expanded further in the chapter, but, to summarise, you will need to do the following:

1. Determine that you have received a valid request for information.
2. Log the request if you have, and provide a receipt. Steps 1 and 2 may be reversed if that is the policy your organization has agreed to. In practice, I find that an obvious non-request does not need logging and the time otherwise spent logging the request can be put to better use.
3. Determine who will have the information and forward the request to them. This includes:
   - forwarding the request to others who may need to see it, e.g. external communications staff. Again, this will depend on your agreed organizational procedures.
4. Manage requests for clarification or scoping of the request that staff might have – this is the duty to advise and assist, section 16 of the FoIA and section 15 of the FoISA. This could include:
   - where staff simply do not understand what is being requested;

   - where the amount of information requested is obviously going to breach the cost limit but a smaller amount of information could be made available;
   - where the number of years of information recorded is less than the number of years of information requested, for example, back to 2000, when recording started only in 2004;
   - where the request looks reasonable but simply does not match the way the information is recorded.

5. Provide staff with the response from the requester relating to clarification. Remember to change the response date as required by how long it took to receive clarification.
6. Remind staff who have otherwise not provided the information that the request will be due in a week's time. Then a day's time, then on the day. And sometimes the day and week after it was due. If the requester chases up the response, forward it to the recalcitrant staff member and do not be afraid to escalate it to managers if you are getting no response from them.
   - If it is possible that a request will not be responded to on the due date, get the department responsible to give you a date by which it can respond and ask the requester if they can wait. Most are happy to do so if it means they will get their information in the end. Technically, this will mean that your organization has responded late to the request, but at least you have kept the requester informed.
7. Package the information/arguments involving exemptions provided by the staff into a response or draft a 'do not hold' response or a combination thereof. Templates are very useful as they contain the basic clauses that you need, including the rights to internal review and complaint to the ICO or SIC.

Covered in Chapter 3 (only point 8 relates solely to exemptions):

8. If you are using an exemption/exemptions, ask staff for arguments as to why the exemption applies, and for the public interest test and/or prejudice test if these apply. Trying to come up with these arguments on your own can be difficult, and you have to write the response in the knowledge that it could be brought before the internal reviewer, the ICO/SIC, the

Information Tribunal and other courts. It can be difficult to get a decent argument out of staff who are not used to thinking in this way, but you have to try to do so in order to ensure that your organization has the best possible response for a regulatory and legal audience.

9 Get sign-off for the request. Again, your organization's procedures may vary. This will normally be someone senior to you, but it cannot be the internal reviewer. Sign-off is actually quite useful. It provides a second pair of eyes to both the information and the response and it can check that you have actually answered the questions asked and pick up whether there are any issues with the response.
   - If you are using the section 36 exemption, this will need to be signed off by the qualified person.

10 Send out the response. This is probably the most satisfying part of the process.
   - Publish the response, edited of personal details, on a disclosure log if you have one.

11 Deal with any minor follow-ups relating to the request. Sometimes requesters have minor follow-up questions, or want to clarify part of the response. If they are asking for new information, start the process at 1 again.

12 Manage the internal review process, particularly if the internal reviewer prefers you to deal with the administrative side of this. Log that the internal review has been done and when the response date is and send reminders as the response date comes closer. The recommended response time for internal reviews is 20 working days for the FoIA. The FoISA section 21 legally requires that 20 working days are taken. The internal reviewer will need to send out the response, but it is best to keep a record yourself of both the internal review request and response. I keep a separate folder for internal reviews, but you may prefer to keep the original request and internal review together.

13 Manage complaints made to the ICO/SIC. This will include drafting your organization's response, bundling together information to send to the ICO/SIC, liaising with your organization's solicitors. Again, I keep a separate folder for these, but you may prefer to keep the original request, internal review and ICO/SIC complaint together in one folder.

14 Manage your participation in preparing for and acting as a witness in an Information Tribunal or other court cases relating to the request.

You are encouraged to read the relevant sections of the FoIA/FoISA. Being able to refer to the correct section of the Act can be very helpful, both for providing the correct response and for managing staff so that they do not claim an exemption that simply does not apply. Knowing exactly what the Act says will help your responses to better comply with the law and will help you to tease out the arguments you need from your colleagues if information is being withheld. The ICO/SIC guidance is helpful, but it is the legislation that you have to comply with so that your responses will not be easy for the ICO/SIC and the courts to pull apart. The more work you put in at the response stage, the less you will have to do later.

The right to information: section 1

Both the FoIA and the FoISA have a similar basis for the right to request information in the very first sections of both Acts. The FoIA section 1(1) states:

> Any person making a request for information to a public authority is entitled—
> (a) to be informed in writing by the public authority whether it holds information of the description specified in the request, and
> (b) if that is the case, to have that information communicated to him.[1]

The FoISA is briefer in its section 1(1), which states:

> A person who requests information from a Scottish public authority which holds it is entitled to be given it by the authority.[2]

Section 1(2) of the FoISA states that a requester should be referred to as an 'applicant'. There is no such requirement in the FoIA, so you can call a requester whatever you like, but I suggest not putting pejorative terms in writing, as it could be requested.

Both Acts allow for a public authority to request further information in order to process a request.[3] Both also limit requests to information held at the time of the request.[4] The issue of whether information is held is discussed below. First, you need to know how to identify if you have received a valid request for information in the first instance.

Identifying a request: section 8

While some countries require that a requester mentions the relevant legislation in the request, the UK and Scottish Acts do not. In order to determine that you have received a valid FoI request, the relevant section is section 8, which states:

> (1) In this Act any reference to a "request for information" is a reference to such a request which—
> (a) is in writing,
> (b) states the name of the applicant and an address for correspondence, and
> (c) describes the information requested.
> (2) For the purposes of subsection (1)(a), a request is to be treated as made in writing where the text of the request—
> (a) is transmitted by electronic means,
> (b) is received in legible form, and
> (c) is capable of being used for subsequent reference.[5]

So, the request must be in writing, give a name and address for correspondence and describe the information requested. These requirements are discussed in more detail below.

As section 8(2)(a) makes clear, e-mail can be used to make a request and an e-mail address is considered to be the same as a postal address. The FoISA is almost word for word the same, except that its section 8(1)(a) allows for 'another form which, by reason of its having some permanency, is capable of being used for subsequent reference (as, for example, a recording made on audio or video tape)'.[6] This has led to the SIC producing guidance on requests left on voicemail, which the ICO has not had to deal with.[7] However, this guidance could be useful to other parts of the UK when dealing with Environmental Information requests (see Chapter 7).

> Can a requester waive their right to FoI, so as to have their request considered outside the scope of either Act? Not according to the SIC, who found in Decision 061/2014, Mr Peter Burke and Angus Council, that although the applicant stated he had not intended to make an official FoI request and it was the Council that had turned it into one,[8] the conditions in section 8 had been met and therefore the Council had acted appropriately in treating the request under the FoISA. If it fits the requirements of section 8, it is an FoI request.

Is it in writing? Section 8(1)(a)

Section 8(1)(a) is fairly clear: either a request is in writing or it is not. It is hard to mistake a verbal request for a written one. However, the format of the request can influence whether it is considered to be legitimately in writing or not. An encrypted request was received by one public authority. This was not considered to meet the requirements of section 8(1)(a) because the public authority could not open it and the requester refused to provide another version.[9] It is possible that a request received in a language other than English (or Welsh, if that applies) would pass the test in this section, but then fail to pass the test in section 8(1)(c), as it would not describe the information well enough for the public authority to provide it.

It is easy to refuse a request which is formatted in a way you cannot access, but what about attachments that could be potentially dangerous? Some ransomware attacks have occurred after people have opened attachments that they thought were legitimate. If you are suspicious about an attachment, you could request that the text of the request be sent within the body of an e-mail; however, this has not been tested with the ICO or in court.

Does it have a name and address for correspondence? Section 8(1)(b)

That an e-mail address is considered an address for correspondence is confirmed by section 8(2). However, does a requester have to use their real name? Can they make an anonymous request or must they provide a real name, with proof of identification?

You must remember that release under FoI is release to the public domain. If you would release the information to another third party, you cannot withhold it from a requester because you do not like what they might do with it. For example, you cannot withhold information from a journalist if you would be happy to provide it to a local resident. FoI is meant to be applicant blind. However, there may be times when you have received a request with an obvious pseudonym, or a requester has provided only a first name or initials. You can consider requesting proof of identity in this situation, as technically this does not meet the test in section 8(1)(b).[10] A legitimate requester will be happy to supply identification on request. However, if you would release the information anyway, then the easiest course of action would be to release it. You cannot request identifying information where the requester has provided their real name.[11]

The ICO guidance on section 8(2)(b) has changed over the years, mainly due to how the Information Tribunal has judged this, as shown in Ghafoor.[12] A tweeter named Bilal Ghafoor, who used the Twitter handle @FoIKid, had used Twitter to request information relating to a Department of Work and Pensions tweet about their Universal Jobsearch programme. Mr Ghafoor requested that the information be tweeted back to him. (This particular case's effect on how you can respond will be dealt with below.)

According to the Information Tribunal, using a Twitter handle did not meet the requirements of section 8 on several grounds. Firstly, the Information Tribunal stated outright that a public authority 'is entitled to know the real name'[13] of a requester, pointing out that the text of the Act refers to '"the" name of the requester'.[14] It also stated that in its opinion, an address of correspondence has to be suitable for carrying out that correspondence.[15] Twitter was not considered an address for correspondence, as it was neither suitable for carrying out the correspondence because it allowed for only 140 characters,[16] nor did it include Mr Ghafoor's real name.[17] Although Mr Ghafoor's name was easily findable within his profile, the Tribunal found that it is not a requirement that a public authority has to look for a requester's real name: this has to be provided directly by the requester themselves.[18]

The following summarises what you need to know about section 8(2)(b):

- The ICO/SIC emphasis is on being applicant blind.
- However, a pseudonym, initials or only a first name are not considered to meet the conditions in section 8(1)(b).

- You can request identification in the above circumstances, and refuse the request if this is not provided.
- You cannot request identification if a real name has been provided.
- However, if you would normally release the information requested, do so even with an obvious pseudonym.

Does it describe the information requested? Section 8(1)(c)

If you are able to determine, from text of the request, what information is required, then this test has been met. If you are not able to identify the likely information, the test will not be met.

This will not necessarily mean refusing the request outright. If the request is somewhat ambiguous, you are required under the advise and assist provisions (section 16) to ask the requester to provide further information so that you can determine what information you hold. For example, if you are asked for a year's worth of information, does the requester mean calendar year, financial year, your financial year if this is different from the norm, academic year, etc.? Both the FoIA and FoISA stop the 20-working days clock until you have received the clarification from the requester.[19] Sometimes it might seem obvious to you what is meant if a colleague requests clarification on a request, but it is better to make the request for clarification and get the answer. There is no time limit on a requester responding with a clarification, although most will respond the same day or soon after.

You can refuse to respond if you are being asked for an opinion[20] or explanation[21] rather than for information per se. This will depend on the details of the request. Questions of the type 'Can you explain to me why …' or 'What does the organization think it was doing about x' are fairly obvious, but sometimes it will be harder to determine. So, consider whether you should seek clarification, although this may not always help. South Wales Police were asked for information about particular security cameras. Although they had indicated that risk assessments were available relating to the cameras, the requester asked the question 'Why is the positioning of these cameras deemed appropriate as both are in contravention of the rules'.[22] The ICO decided that this was not describing information requested but seeking 'justification for and explanation of [the requester's] allegation'.[23] The

ICO has even decided in one case that a request that appeared vexatious was simply not a valid request in the first place.[24]

Whether questions that led to a yes/no answer were valid was looked at by the SIC in Decision 073/2015. The SIC found that these types of questions were valid if the yes or no could be generated from the information held.[25]

However, do not attempt to dismiss a request because it just asks for 'documents' or 'e-mails'. While both Acts refer to information, both the ICO and SIC have dismissed arguments that a reference to 'documents' does not fit within the test for describing information requested.[26]

> In FS50465008, the ICO rejected the Cabinet Office's argument that requesting the last e-mail sent from the Prime Minister's account did not adequately describe the content of the e-mail and therefore was not describing the information. Describing the e-mail required was information enough without needing to know what it contained: 'there is no requirement in the FOIA that those intending to make requests for information have any prior knowledge of the information they are requesting'.[27]

The following summarises what you need to know about section 8(1)(c):

- If you can identify the information requested, the request passes the test in section 8(1)(c).
- If you can partially identify it but need clarification, contact the requester for clarification based on the requirements of section 16.
- You can reject requests which are asking for opinion and/or explanation.
- You cannot reject requests asking for e-mails, documents, files, folders but that do not necessarily mention subjects.

Other 'electronic means'

Other electronic means covers, for example, social media like Facebook, Twitter or other text-based communications. These are considered legitimate means of making an FoI request, as they are written and they have an address – either the Facebook name or

Twitter handle – to respond to. The ICO guidance has always been that they can be used to make an FoI request, with the proviso added in the most recent guidance that the requester has to have their real name somewhere in their profile.[28] A public authority can use another method for the response, for example e-mail, if it would be impossible to include the information requested in a tweet.

Logging the request

Having decided that you have received a relevant request, you will need to track it. There are different logging systems available; for example, JISC[29] has an Information Request Register[30] and there are commercial systems as well.[31] Whether your organization has the funds for a commercial system or you decide to track using a spreadsheet or some other system, you should do the following:

1 Use a unique number for each request. This will help to track them, particularly if you have a complaint about multiple requests that goes to the ICO/SIC.
2 Determine dates for response. This is not just the date of response for the request, but the date of response for internal reviews, the date for responding to the ICO, etc.
3 Track the date when you responded. As above, including the dates when you responded to internal reviews, etc.
4 Include the information requested. This helps when trying to identify previous requests on the same topics.
5 Include to whom you forwarded the request.
6 Provide management information about requests. It is likely that you will need to provide your senior management with data about the requests received and how you are managing them.[32] Some suggestions for data to collect are:
   a time periods for response. For example, up to 5 days, 5–10 days, 11–15 days, 16–20 days, late. This helps to identify how often you do not meet the deadline, and helps also in tracking the types of requests that are taking the most time to respond to;
   b how you responded, for example, fully, partially, refused due to exemption, refused as vexatious, information not held, etc.;

c what exemptions, if any, you used. Do not forget section 12, the cost limit, in this list;
d request category – for example, human resources, finance, management and administration, policy and procedures, etc.;
e requester category – for example, journalist, commercial organization, contractor, staff member, etc.

A good logging system will be able to provide reminders when a request is close to being due, but you may have to use reminders in your calendar system instead.

How to determine a response date: section 10

In the FoIA, section 10(1) states:

> Subject to subsections (2) and (3), a public authority must comply with section 1(1) promptly and in any event not later than the twentieth working day following the date of receipt.[33]

A 'working day' is defined as: 'any day other than a Saturday, a Sunday, Christmas Day, Good Friday or a day which is a bank holiday under the Banking and Financial Dealings Act 1971 in any part of the United Kingdom'.[34]

The FoISA is similar, although adds a subsection that 'twenty working days' applies from the receipt of clarification if this is requested.[35] However, the inclusion of 'promptly' suggests that waiting until day 19 to request clarification and then taking another 20 days to respond is likely to be frowned upon. The same definition of working day is used.[36]

So, if a request comes in on 1 November when this is a weekday, you would have to respond by 29 November. However, if you receive it on 10 December, 20 working days is likely to mean a response date of 3 or 4 January, once you have included the weekends, Christmas Day, Boxing Day, New Year's Day and any bank holidays if those days fall on a weekend. Any requests received on any of the non-working days listed above will have the next working day as their starting point. So, for a request sent on a Saturday, the clock starts on Monday, unless that is a bank holiday, in which case it would be Tuesday.

Although different bank holidays apply in different parts of the UK, any bank holidays anywhere in the UK are considered non-working days in all parts of the UK. So, all of us could take St Patrick's day as a non-working day for FoI purposes, even though it is a bank holiday only in Northern Ireland.[37] However, you may decide to ignore the bank holidays outside your particular country, for simplicity's sake.

The length of a working day was dealt with in the case *Berend v ICO & London Borough of Richmond upon Thames* (EA/2006/0049), which states in paragraph 63: 'There is no definition within the Act as to the length of a day and in the absence of any such definition, we are satisfied that a day ends at midnight.'[38] So, it is only requests received past midnight that can be said to have been received the next working day.

For how to handle the time changes for requests for confirmation see the section below, 'Requesting clarification and defining scope'. Also, if you are considering the public interest in an exemption, you can take a further 20 working days to determine the public interest test, which is discussed in Chapter 3.

Sending a receipt

Do you have to provide a receipt confirming that you have received the request? Strictly speaking, there is nothing in either Act that requires this, so it depends on your organization's policy. You may decide to send a receipt:

- for every request received;
- only when it is requested; and/or
- only when a request has been received elsewhere in the organization and been referred to you.

Is it really our request?

If you receive a request where you are not the relevant public authority, but you know who is, you can transfer the request. You have two choices at this point. The first is to forward the request to the authority and let the requester know you have done so. The second is to tell the requester whom they should contact and let them do so themselves. Either is considered valid.

Determining who has the information and forwarding the request to them

You know that big red button that you press to automatically produce the information requested? Nor do I. Even if you have an electronic document and records management system, the likelihood is that you will have to ask another staff member to provide you with the information requested, if only because they will understand the context around the information in a way that you do not. You will find that some information is obviously in the domain of one individual or team; for example, information about information technology (IT) contracts is likely to be with your IT department. Some requests will even cover multiple parts of your organization; for example, universities may receive requests for information held in every faculty or department. There will also be times when you really do not have a clue who to contact and will have to ask around to find out to whom to send the request. It is important to have your personal networks set up in your organization so that you can navigate to the place where the requested information is kept.

Section 12, the cost limit

You may have concerns about the amount of information requested and think there may be a breach of the cost limit in section 12 (the text is different but the section number is the same in both the FoIA and FoISA; both sections also allow the aggregation of two or more requests on the same topic when considering if the cost limit applies), which in the Freedom of Information and Data Protection (Appropriate Limit and Fees) Regulations referred to in section 12 of the FoIA equates to 24 hours of work in central government and 18 in other parts of the public sector. This is calculated via the following: the Freedom of Information and Data Protection (Appropriate Limit and Fees) Regulations 2004 No. 3244 states in Regulation 3(2) that the appropriate limit is £600 for FoIA Schedule 1, Part 1 public authorities. Regulation 3(3) gives £450 as the appropriate limit for other public authorities. Regulation 4(4) sets the hourly cost per person as £25. Hence 600/25 equates to 24 hours, while 450/25 equates to 18 hours. The equivalent Scottish regulations set a limit of 40 hours.[39] This will be discussed in greater detail below, but it is worth alerting staff when you forward the request to them if you think that section 12 might apply.

If there is a possibility that you would want to release the information anyway, section 13 allows you to request that a fee is paid for the information that would otherwise be exempt from release under section 12.

Global searches

You may receive a request, for example, to search for every e-mail on a particular topic. Depending on how your systems are set up, this may not be possible. For example, previous versions of Microsoft Exchange did not allow for this and every mailbox would have needed to be searched. Cloud-based systems, however, allow for greater searching capabilities and can allow searches over the entire cloud domain.

Your organization should already have a procedure for managing requests for information in the mailboxes of staff who are not in the office due to sickness or other absence. You will need a similar procedure for these sorts of requests for global searches. Make sure that you include in the procedure how to determine the search string, as common words and phrases will result in too much 'noise' being returned in the search. For example, 'Freedom of Information Act' is likely to bring back better search results than 'information' would. There may be times when you can refuse a request because the search string provided is not specific enough. It will be part of your duty to advise and assist (see below, 'Requesting clarification and defining scope') to ensure that you are given a search string that provides what the requester wants but does not result in too many false positives.

You will have to review the search results (probably provided by your IT department) for any personal data before sending out. Depending on your procedure, you will need to let staff know that the material from their mailboxes has been included in the response to the request.

Forwarding the request

Some organizations remove the requester's details (name and contact details) before forwarding the request, so as to keep the identity of the request applicant blind. However, it is arguable that the Acts themselves require this. It interferes in the ability to identify requests that are vexatious or that may need to be aggregated. Staff tend to be more comfortable in dealing with a request if they can guess what the requester is likely to do with the information. FoI takes control away from staff: that is its point. It is meant to allow a member of the public to request information without needing to provide a reason why. However, in my experience, if staff feel that they understand why the information is requested:

a the helpful ones will provide useful clarification on what their systems hold and how best to meet the request, in the spirit as well as in the letter of the request;
b the less helpful ones will feel that they have some control over the information they are sending out, rather than feeling that it is going out into a void;
c the completely unhelpful ones need the sticks of 'you could be fined if you don't provide the info requested', although this was more necessary when the FoIA was first implemented.

So, there are pros and cons to including the name of the requester as well as other identifying information. If you do decide to remove the identifying information, you may have to provide it to colleagues if they believe the requester could be vexatious. It is also worth remembering that the requester does not have to supply a reason for requesting the information, even if your colleagues want to guess at one.

Whom else to include

You may want or be asked to include communications staff when forwarding the request, when the response is drafted, or both, so that they are aware of what is being requested and what information has been provided in the event that there are press enquiries relating to the request. Possibly they will want to see only those requests relating to journalists. This can be helpful, as communications staff can be aware of a wider picture relating to the request and may have some useful turns of phrase to help in forming the response. However, you must keep in mind that communications staff tend to feel a duty to protect the organization by controlling what information is provided to outsiders. This cannot be allowed to overrule the legal requirement to provide the information requested. Providing a full response to an information request is also a form of protection for the organization, as it shows responsibility and good citizenship. So, be prepared to push back as necessary on a suggestion from communications staff.

Other staff who may want to be included are managers. They may be happy for their staff to actually handle the request, but will want to keep an eye on what is coming in and going out.

It is worth keeping a note somewhere of all your contacts and rules relating to different departments and teams, so that if you are unavailable and someone else has to take over, they can do so smoothly.

Requesting clarification and defining scope: section 16/15 duty to advise and assist

Some requests are obviously unclear, for example, requesting a year's worth of information but not specifying the year, where 'year' could mean calendar year, financial year, academic year, etc. Others may seem clear on receipt but simply do not match the way information is held. Some may be clear, but be asking for too much information, and so could potentially be covered by the cost limit in section 12. As such, having forwarded the request, you may find that it returns to you because your colleague(s) cannot understand the request or provide all the data requested within the time limit, or wants clarification from the requester before they can provide the information. This is covered by section 1(3) and section 16 of the FoIA/section 15 of the FoISA.

Section 1(3) of the FoIA states:

> Where a public authority—
> (a) reasonably requires further information in order to identify and locate the information requested, and
> (b) has informed the applicant of that requirement,
> the authority is not obliged to comply with subsection (1) unless it is supplied with that further information.[40]

This also fits with the duty to advise and assist in section 16, which states:

> Duty to provide advice and assistance.
> (1) It shall be the duty of a public authority to provide advice and assistance, so far as it would be reasonable to expect the authority to do so, to persons who propose to make, or have made, requests for information to it.
> (2) Any public authority which, in relation to the provision of advice or assistance in any case, conforms with the code of practice under section 45 is to be taken to comply with the duty imposed by subsection (1) in relation to that case.[41]

The Freedom of Information (Scotland) Act 2002, asp 13, section 15 is more or less the same, except that it refers to Scottish public authorities in section 15(1), and the section 60 code of practice in section 15(2).

What this means in practice is that you need to communicate with a requester as soon as possible, telling them:

- what is unclear and/or
- what information you can provide within the cost limit.

It is worth stressing to colleagues that if there are any issues or need for clarification, they should get back to you as soon as possible. If you wait until day 18 to get clarification, you will have only two days left to process the request after receiving it.

Response time changes

If you have requested confirmation, the 20 working days clock then stops until the requester comes back to you with the confirmation. This needs to be logged. If enough time has passed, you may also need to seek confirmation on whether to respond with the information you hold now rather than that held at the time when the request was originally made.

If you are unable to provide the information requested within the cost limit, but have agreed a smaller scope of request with the requester, this is technically a new request and the 20 working days start again. Technically, when you do this you are refusing the first request under section 12. However, depending on how quickly the requester confirms that they are happy with the new scope, you may end up with the same response deadline anyway.

Once you have worked out and logged the new response deadlines, forward the clarification or the redefined scope of the request to your colleagues as quickly as you can after you have received it, including notification of the new response deadlines.

What happens if you do not receive a response? You can wait until the original response deadline to move the request correspondence into an archival space, but requesters have been known to return more than six months later, so always be ready to respond to a late confirmation.

Fees

Aside from the cost limit, you are allowed to charge for disbursements, like photocopying or postage.[42] Having worked out what this would cost, you have to send a fees notice to the requester setting out the fee and the reasons for it. I have sent one fees notice in my 12 years of dealing with FoI requests, but if you work in an archive or with large paper collections, you need to have a policy on how much to charge for photocopying and postage, and to ensure that it is in line with the fees regulations.

Inability to meet a request response date

Some areas of the organization will have particular times of the year that are pressure points. They will be so busy getting their work done that processing an FoI request will be too much for them. While it will still leave you technically in breach of section 1(1) of the Acts, let the requester know about the difficulty and see if you can agree a date for response that is not too far from the 20 working days response date. I have found that requesters are usually happy to wait if it means that they will get the information they want at some point.

Be careful with this, as you cannot do this with every requester without ending up with, at the very least, a practice recommendation from the Information Commissioner. It does have to be a legitimate need on behalf of your colleagues. And if it is likely that an exemption would have to be used, say so as soon as possible, rather than putting off the requester, as waiting longer than normal only to be told that you cannot have the information will just add insult to injury. The point is to try to avoid a complaint to the ICO, not provoke one.

Reminders

The FoI Officer (you may have a different title, but this is about the role) is the point at which a requester and the organization meet. As such, it is your role to act as the requester's champion as far as possible while at the same time discharging your organization's legal responsibilities in a way that does not cause damage to the organization. As the requester's champion, part of your role is to remind your colleagues when a request is due, so that the requester gets their information in a timely fashion. This also helps the organization by ensuring that staff enable it to meet its legal responsibilities.

So, be prepared to send reminders. A week before the due date gives enough time to allow a staff member to provide the information in time. The text can be a simple 'This is a reminder that this request is due'. However, if you have most of the information for a response but are waiting on one person, it is worth copying and pasting the questions that they specifically have to answer into the reminder e-mail so they do not have to go looking for them.

The next reminder to send is on the final day. If it looks like you will not get the response out that day, you can communicate this to the requester so they will know it will be late. You will still be, strictly speaking, in breach of the Act, but at least you have not left the requester in the dark as to what is happening.

Once you have gone past the response date, you will need to consider if you need to escalate the request to your colleague's manager. You may also have to keep sending reminders until responding to you is less painful than having another e-mail pop up about the request again.

Drafting the response and sign-off

Responses can be one or a combination of the following:

- providing the information requested;
- notifying the requester that the organization does not have the information requested;
- notifying the requester that the information requested is exempt;
- notifying the requester that the request is repeated or vexatious.

Depending on your organization, you may have a policy of sending out responses directly after they have been drafted, or you may have to get sign-off from a senior manager. It is required that the qualified person signs off on a request as part of the process for using the exemption in section 36 (see Chapter 3). While it does add to the response time, sign-off allows for a second pair of eyes to look at the response and check that it does fit the request. It also gives senior managers oversight of the information that is being released so that they can deal with any follow-ups like complaints, media attention, campaigns, etc.

Templates are useful for responses, as they will have all the clauses that you need for the response. Aside from the information, or the reason why you have not provided it, you need to include your contact details in case there is a problem. You also need to include the details of your internal review process, and it is a requirement to include a link to the ICO when using an exemption under the FoIA.[43] You may also want to include a sentence or paragraph on your re-use of public sector information process as well, if you are subject to the Re-use of Public Sector Information Regulations 2005 No. 1515 and/or a copyright notice.

Providing the information requested

This is the easiest response to make and (hopefully) less likely to lead to a complaint than any of the others. The main issue is to ensure that you have definitely provided the information requested. When you receive this from the staff who hold it, check that it really does answer the questions asked. If the information does differ slightly because that is what the organization holds, or because context is needed, provide an explanation along with the information. It happens that sometimes it is only at this stage that you find out that the information held does not quite match the request, so do use the duty to advise and assist to meet the request as closely as possible, while pointing to alternative information that exists and can be provided in your response.

If you get a follow-up to a response providing information, you will need to decide whether to handle it as an extension to the request – for example, 'should the column in tab 3 say x rather than y' – or a completely new request – such as, 'thanks for the information, can you provide the same figures for department A'. It depends whether completely new information is being asked for, which makes it a new request, or just clarification on the information you have provided.

Technically, the relevant section 1(1) of the FoIA states you have to say that you hold the information, and then provide it if you do; but obviously, if you are providing it you are by implication communicating that you hold it.

Refusing the request due to information not held

This is covered by a specific section of the FoISA, section 17. There is no such section in the UK FoIA: section 1(1)(a) covers communicating if information is held or not. These are also easy responses, because if you do not hold the information, you cannot provide it. For example, how much money do you raise in car park charges when you do not have a car park? You do have to be certain that this is actually the case, and sometimes it may be that the information is held in a way that makes it hard to extract. In this case, section 12 is more likely to apply, rather than information not held (see Chapter 3 for an explanation of section 12). Unlike providing the information, you may get a request for an internal review for these responses.

Conclusion

Now that you have finished this chapter, you should know:

- how to manage requests for information;
- how to recognise a request;
- how to determine if a request is a legitimate request under the FoIA and FoISA;
- how to log requests, including working out time periods;
- to whom to send requests internally;

- why you might need to request clarification and how;
- how and why to send internal reminders;
- how to draft a response – remembering to answer the questions!

For guidance on the cost limit, vexatious and repeated requests and using an exemption, see Chapter 3.

3

Freedom of information exemptions

Introduction

This chapter focuses on the exemptions available under the UK Freedom of Information Act (FoIA) and the Freedom of Information (Scotland) Act (FoISA). They are covered in order of the FoIA, but any section number differences are included in Table 3.1 so that if you work for a Scottish public authority you can find the right section more easily.

The first section covers what you have to consider when applying an exemption, which also includes whether you have to apply the public interest test or prejudice test. Both of these are explained below. Each exemption is discussed, with the particular issues to look out for when you are thinking of applying the exemption. If you are new to Freedom of Information (FoI), you will find this section more useful. Those with more experience may prefer to head straight to the exemption guidance.

Covered in this chapter are:

- the exemptions and how to apply them;
- dealing with internal reviews;
- dealing with complaints to the Information Commissioner's Office (ICO) and Scottish Information Commissioner (SIC);
- managing the publication scheme.

Covered in Chapter 2 are:

- the basic method for handling a request, which is also useful for the EIR;
- how to recognise a request;
- how to process a request;
- how to handle requests for clarification;
- how to create a response.

As in Chapter 2, when I refer to 'you' I am thinking of the records manager or information manager who finds themselves in the position of having to manage responses to FoI requests. You can read through the whole of both chapters or dip into the parts that have the most relevance. I suggest reading through all the exemptions at least once to ensure that you are familiar with them all. You will use certain exemptions many times, but others very rarely. It is worth knowing about those other ones for the few occasions when you need them.

Refusing the request due to an exemption

Section 17 of the FoIA and section 16 of the FoISA set out the requirements of a refusal notice. The two sections are similar, but not the same. For both, a public authority is required to:

- state that the information is held;
- state that the information is exempt from release and which exemption(s) applies;
- explain why the exemption has been applied, if this is not clear;
- include arguments on how the public interest test or prejudice test were conducted for the exemptions that require them.

Where the two Acts differ is on whether a public authority can neither confirm nor deny that they hold information. For the FoIA, this is applicable to all exemptions, whether they are absolute exemptions or, for the public interest test exemptions, when it is in the public interest to neither confirm nor deny.[1] For the FoISA, only certain exemptions allow a public authority to neither confirm nor deny that the information exists.[2]

If you are new to FoI, you may wonder why you would want to neither confirm nor deny that information exists. Mainly, this is because even knowing the information exists or does not exist would be information in and of itself. For example, to refuse to release an investigation report would confirm that an investigation had taken place. To say that you do not hold an investigation report is also confirming that there was no investigation. If that investigation related to one individual, or to a national security incident, and there was no information already in the public domain, you would be confirming information about the individual or incident just by saying you do or do not hold the information.

Table 3.1 (on pages 40–1) lists the exemptions available in each Act, most of which occur in both the FoIA and FoISA, although the FoIA has a couple more and certain sections of the FoISA contain two exemptions that have their own sections in the FoIA.

Applying the exemptions requires the following:

1 identifying an exemption that applies, which can sometimes be difficult even when it seems obvious the information is exempt; for example, it is hard to identify an obvious exemption for information security concerns. Yemen's FoI Act includes an exemption for information: Article 25 (F) 'The electronic information which, if disclosed, could cause penetration of protected networks and equipment and may expose them to deletion or theft'.[3] Unfortunately, this is not available in the FoIA and FoISA;
2 checking the text of the exemption to be certain that you can apply it to the particular information you want to exempt. At this point it is also worth checking whether you should neither confirm nor deny the information exists;
3 unless the exemption is absolute, applying the public interest test. That means, even if the information does fit within the exemption, is it still in the public interest to release it? Any time that you apply a public interest test exemption, you should include some explanatory text on how you applied the test;
4 if the exemption mentions prejudice – which means would there be any harm to the public authority, an individual or another group in releasing this information – considering what this harm would be and whether it is substantial enough for the exemption to apply;

5 considering if any exemptions with particular tests – for example, the personal data exemption and prejudice to the effective conduct of public affairs relating to those exemptions – apply.

Where more than one exemption could apply, you have to go through the above for all of them. If you are using an exemption for the first time or have not used a particular exemption for some time, it would be worth reading the ICO/SIC guidance on the exemption. It will also be helpful to look at the decisions handed down by the ICO/SIC and the Information Tribunal and other courts to see whether the arguments you intend to use have not already been dismissed. In particular, pay attention to the decisions made relating to your sector. And, although as a UK public authority you are not subject to the SIC decisions (and vice versa for Scottish public authorities), it is still helpful to look at their decisions, as similar arguments could be used when the exemptions are identical or aligned together.

Table 3.1 *Exemptions in the FoIA and FoISA: similarities and differences*

Exemption	FoIA section	FoISA section	Public interest?	Prejudice test?
Cost limit	12	12	No	No
Information already accessible	21	25	No	No
Information due for publication	22	27(1) – with 12 week limitation	Yes	No
Research	22A	27(2)	Yes	Yes
Information supplied to or relating to security bodies	23	N/A	No	No
National security	24	31(1)–(3)	Yes	No
Defence	26	31(4)	Yes	No
International relations	27	32	Yes	Yes, both, though FoISA has to substantially prejudice
Relations within the UK	28	28	Yes	Yes, both, though FoISA has to substantially prejudice
The economy	29	33(2)	Yes	Yes, both, though FoISA has to substantially prejudice

(*Continued*)

Table 3.1 *Continued*

Exemption	FoIA section	FoISA section	Public interest?	Prejudice test?
Investigations and proceedings conducted by a [Scottish] public authority	30	34	Yes	No
Law enforcement	31	35	No	Yes, both, though FoISA has to substantially prejudice
Court records, etc.	32	37	No	No
Audit functions	33	40	Yes	Yes, both, though FoISA has to substantially prejudice
Parliamentary privilege	34	No equivalent	No	No
Formulation of government/Scottish administration policy	35	29	Yes	No
Prejudice to the effective conduct of public affairs	36	No equivalent	Partial	Yes
Communications with Her Majesty, etc. and Honours	37	41	Partial	No
Health and safety	38	39(1)	Yes	No
Environmental information	39	39(2)	Yes	No
Personal information	40	38	Yes	Yes
Information provided in confidence/confidentiality	41	36(2)	No	Yes
Legal professional privilege	42	36(1)	Yes	Yes
Commercial interests	43	33	Yes	Yes
Prohibitions on disclosure	44	26	No	No

These exemptions are covered below in FoIA section order. If you work for a Scottish public authority, Table 3.1 will help you to navigate to the right part of the chapter. For each section, you will find points that you need to cover or consider in your response. These can help you to guide the staff who hold the information to provide you with the arguments that you need in order to use the exemption.

Section 12, The cost limit

Both section 12s reference the fees regulations[4] that determine how much work would need to be done before the cost limit kicks in and a request can be refused. The cost limit is £600 for FoIA Schedule 1 Part 1 public authorities, that is, central government, legislative bodies and the armed forces, with some exceptions and additions, and £450 for all other UK public authorities. The cost per hour set in each of the Regulations is £25 for the FoIA fees regulations and £15 for the FoISA fees regulations. This means that in order to refuse a request due to the cost limit:

- if you are in a UK central government department, legislative body or the armed forces, you must reach 24 hours' work;
- if you are any other UK public authority, you must reach 18 hours' work;
- if you are a Scottish public authority, you must reach 40 hours' work.

When calculating the cost of the response, you cannot include the time taken to decide on exemptions, although there is scope with the public interest test exemptions to take a further 20 working days if necessary to focus on the public interest in the information. Also, you cannot include redacting information in most of the UK, but can include time taken for redaction if you work for a Scottish public authority. You can include searching for the information and extracting it, including getting it back from off-site storage. You are not required to do a detailed, precise estimate for how long it would take, but it is useful to scope what you would have to do in order to provide the information. For example, the information is somewhere in the paper files stored in basement room x, it would take five minutes to pull these off the shelf, look through the file for the information, copy the information and replace the file on the shelf. While your response does not necessarily have to provide a full account of what you would have to do to search for the information, do press your colleagues for some details, because if there is a complaint to the ICO you will have to provide this information when responding to it.

While you can refuse an entire request if one or more parts breach the cost limit, in practice it is better to provide what you can and use the cost limit only for the part(s) of a request for which you really cannot provide the data within the limit. However, you can include the work that you do to meet those parts of the request you can fit within the cost limit within your calculations, for example, it took one hour to produce the responses to questions 1, 2 and 3, so that leaves 23/17/39 hours for question 4.

Section 21 (FoIA)/25 (FoISA), Information already available

The key to this exemption is that the information is readily accessible to the requester. So, if the information is on a website, in a publication or otherwise already in the public domain, you can use this exemption. If the information is on a website, you should provide a web link, particularly if it is hard to find the information on your website. It saves dealing with follow-up e-mails. You can charge postage for publications if you need to send out a hard copy.[5] If documents are available to view at a particular venue, provide the address or contact details.

If you are using this exemption, you will need to cover the following points:

- If the information is available at a cost, you can require that any fees necessary are paid before providing the information. However, if only a small amount of the information covered by a fee is required, you should consider providing it without requiring the fee.[6]
- You do have to take into account the requester's circumstances. For example, if a document is available for inspection but the requester is disabled and cannot get into the building, the information will not be accessible for them and you will have to provide it.
- There will be some information that is made available under different legislation, for example the Access to Health Records Act[7] or the Antisocial Behaviour Etc. (Scotland) Act 2004.[8] These are discussed in Chapter 8.

Section 22 (FoIA)/27 (FoISA), Information due for publication and research

These sections cover information that is due for publication (section

22/27(1)), and also research (section 22A/27(2)). Section 22/27(1) is covered first, then section 22A/27(2).

Regarding information due for publication, the main difference between the FoIA and FoISA is that for the FoISA the information must be published within 12 weeks of the request. However, this doesn't mean that non-Scottish public authorities can take as much time as they like to respond. The information in question should be on schedule to be published. It is easier to apply the exemption if the information will be published next week rather than next year. This is also a public interest test exemption, so you will need to balance waiting for publication versus releasing the request now. One reason for waiting could be that the publication still needs to go through an internal review process. If it is past that process and simply waiting to be put on a website or published as a paper document, the public interest could be in providing it in response to the request.

If you are using section 22/27(1), you should consider the following points:

- Publication can be made by a third party. It does not have to be the public authority itself.
- Publication means any way in which the information could be made available to the public, for example, as part of an exhibition.
- Does the publication actually contain the information requested? In my own experience, I have found that Annual Accounts may supply some financial information, but this does not always match exactly what is being requested.
- The intent to publish is important and has to be known at the time when the request is made, even if an exact time for publication is not known, due to other factors, e.g. peer review.[9]
- The focus of the public interest test for this exemption is the harm that would occur from releasing earlier than the publication date.

The FoISA contained an exemption for research, section 27(2), from the beginning. Section 22A was added to the FoIA after lobbying from the university sector when the FoIA was reviewed in 2013–14. Both sections allow for 'information obtained in the course of, or derived from a programme of research'[10] to be exempt if to release it would harm the research; and for the FoISA harm has to be substantial, or the interests of anyone involved in the research. Although the two sections are virtually the same, the ICO and SIC guidance differs. The SIC maintains that the research must be published at some point, and if the decision is taken not to publish, then section 27(2) no longer applies to the information. The ICO, however, allows that 'The exemption will include a wide range of information relating to the research project, and will cover information that is not necessarily going to be published. In other words, there does not need to be any intention to publish the information that has been requested.'[11]

When using sections 22A/27(2), you must keep the following points in mind:

- Research is not defined in either Act, but the ICO provides the definition 'a systematic investigation intended to establish facts, acquire new knowledge and reach new conclusions',[12] while the SIC guidance points to the debates on the FoISA bill in the Scottish Parliament relating to academic research being the focus for the FoISA.[13] So, while both exemptions are most likely to be used by universities, other non-Scottish public bodies which produce original research can use section 22A as well.
- The research must be ongoing at the time of the request. For the FoIA, this means that some publication of data may have already occurred but, due to ongoing research, the rest of the information can still be exempted.[14] The SIC guidance makes the point that only finite research is covered – that is, the programme of research has to have an end point.[15]
- The harm to the research itself or to the interests of the public authority or individuals or any other authorities involved has to be more than likely. You will need to demonstrate how release of the information related to the research will damage the research project, or the interests of those involved, or the interests of the public authority. For example, the main fear of academics that led to the exemption was that they could work at creating a dataset for decades and finally be at the point of exploiting it, only to have another academic request the data and publish their findings first. In this case, if the second academic worked in the same subject area, this would be more likely to cause harm to the first academic. If the second academic worked in a related or

completely different area, the harm to publishing first might not be so great.

- The public interest test does apply to these sections, so you will need to consider this as well. It is more likely that it could be in the public interest to release the information requested if the research is particularly controversial.

Sections 23, 24, 25, 26 (FoIA)/section 31 (FoISA), Security bodies, national security and defence

As these exemptions tend to be used together for most organizations that use them, they are discussed together here. The exemptions in the FoIA cover more than those in the FoISA, which has no direct equivalent to sections 23 and 25 of the FoIA. However, its section 31 covers similar information to sections 24 and 26 of the FoIA.

To summarise, section 23 covers information supplied to and relating to the security bodies listed in section 23(3). Section 24 covers information relating to national security that is not covered by section 23. Its FoISA equivalent is section 31(1). Sections 26 and 34(4, 5) cover information relating to defence and the armed forces.

Section 25, which is not listed in Table 3.1, covers supplementary provisions to sections 23(2) and 24(3) about the certificates that can be issued by a Minister of the Crown to certify that the exemptions have been correctly applied. This means that a Minister of the Crown can certify that information is exempt, which is considered sufficient evidence that it is exempt that it would not have to be provided to the ICO/SIC when reviewing a complaint about the exempted information.

More detail on each exemption is provided below, which may be of more use to those public authorities that use them regularly. Generally, if you are not a frequent user of these exemptions, keep the following points in mind:

- Unlike for the exemptions that you use more frequently, you will need to read the text of the Act and the guidance provided by the ICO/SIC carefully to ensure that you are applying the exemption(s) correctly.
- You will have to consider carefully whether neither confirm nor

deny should be applied to the request. If the information is exempt, it is highly possible that even acknowledging its existence could be information in and of itself. This is true also if no information is held.

- If you are using the FoIA, keep in mind the difference between sections 23 and 24.
- If necessary, contact the relevant security body for its advice and opinion relating to the information. This does not necessarily mean that you have to follow it, but it shows the ICO/SIC that you have considered all the angles relating to the request.
- The ICO/SIC both handle complaints relating to these exemptions carefully. They will not investigate further or require that information be provided if a ministerial certificate is provided[16] or if a written assurance from a senior member of a public authority satisfies them that the information should not be divulged. However, if it is less clear cut, they may be required to see the information before making a decision.
- The public interest test may not apply just to current information, but could apply to historical information as well.

If you are using section 23 relating to specific security bodies in the FoIA, keep the following points in mind:

- You need to focus on who supplied the information and which security body it relates to.
- This is a class-based exemption, so no harm to the security body needs to be proved. However, you do need to decide, on a balance of probabilities, what harm the information might do.
- Neither confirm nor deny can be used in place of no information held to ensure that applying the exemption itself does not confirm that information is not held about a particular security body. However, this is easier for some public authorities to use, such as the Home Office, who might be expected to hold such information, as compared to a parish council.[17]

If you need to apply section 24 FoIA/section 31(1) FoISA relating to national security more generally, you need to focus on the following:

- The information relates to national security, which can encompass information relating to military defence, protection of democracy and the workings of the state in co-operation with other states relating to terrorism, or all of the above – not just military security.
- Release of the information needs to have an adverse effect on national security. It cannot just relate to national security for the exemption to apply. However, the threat does not need to be immediate.
- This is a public interest test exemption, but it is likely that the public interest will be to exempt the information. It will be balanced towards release if the information could help the public to comply with measures to protect national security.
- Leaked information may be in the public domain, but still be subject to the exemption.

If you want to apply section 26 FoIA/sections 31(4,5) FoISA to defence and/or armed forces information, you need to cover the following:

- Consider whether the information relates to the functioning of the armed forces, whether in peace time or during defence operations. The exemption covers harm to the defence and/or capability, effectiveness and security of the armed forces.
- Anything which could harm the ability of the armed forces to carry out their duties will likely be covered by these exemptions.

Section 27 (FoIA)/section 32 (FoISA), International relations

Again, this may not be an exemption that a lot of public authorities have to deal with and you may find yourself considering it along with the security and defence exemptions.

There are two tests contained in these exemptions. The first covers whether release of the information would harm relations between the UK and another state, an international court or tribunal and the interests of the UK or promotion and protection of the interests of the UK abroad. The second covers confidential information obtained from another state or international court or tribunal. As with all the prejudice tests for the FoISA, there has to be substantial prejudice for section 32 to apply. The test for confidentiality is covered in more detail below in the discussion on sections 41/36(2).

If you want to apply the international relations exemption, you will need to consider the following points:

- There is the potential for a wide range of information to be included in the exemption, from diplomatic matters to international trade information, controversial visitors to the UK, twinning with other public authorities, research agreements with universities and other bodies outside the UK, etc.[18] It does not just cover diplomatic relations.
- However, you will need to demonstrate harm to relations with a state, international court or tribunal or to the UK's interests before you can apply the exemption. This will depend on the state(s) involved, as some will be more open to sharing information, while others will not. You can also consider harm to UK citizens and business currently in that state.
- This is also a public interest test exemption, so you will have to consider release even if harm can occur. For example, if it is in the public interest to know some of the details relating to negotiations for membership in a group of states, even if release could harm negotiations, it may be in the public interest to release them.

Section 28, Relations within the UK

Scottish public authorities can skip this section, as it has no equivalent in the FoISA. If you are a UK public authority, you may not need to use this exemption much either, unless you have a lot of contact with the devolved authorities.

If you want to apply this exemption, you first have to consider if it relates to relations between the UK government and the Scottish Administration, Welsh and Northern Ireland Assemblies, and then apply the prejudice test and public interest test as you would normally. The overall consideration is: will there be harm to relations between the administrations, the exchange of information or to the ability of both the UK and devolved administration to discharge their duties? Section 28 has generally been used with sections 35 and 36 where there has been overlap between formation of government policy and conduct of public affairs with relation to the devolved administrations, so you should look at both those exemptions as well if you are considering section 28.

This has not been an easy exemption to apply. There are only about half a dozen ICO decision notices at the time of writing where section 28 has been used by a public authority, and most of these were rejected by the ICO.

> The only decision that upheld the use of section 28 related to the Welsh Office.[19] In this case, the letters covered by the exemption showed clearly the disparate views between the UK and Welsh governments that had been discussed frankly. The ICO accepted that release would harm relations between the two and that it was in the public interest to ensure that relations were not harmed.

Section 29 (FoIA)/section 33(2) (FoISA), The economy

This is another prejudice test exemption, with the harm this time focused on the economic interests of the UK or any part of the UK or the financial interests of any administration in the UK. The focus of the first test is on any damage that could cause instability or wider damage to the UK economy.[20] This could include damage to a single company if the impact on that company would be damaging to the UK economy or a part of it more widely.[21] Commercial-in-confidence or trade secrets information will need to be treated separately using section 43, but you may need to consider both exemptions.

The second test is narrower, as it focuses on financial dealings of the UK government, Scottish Administration and the Welsh and Northern Ireland Assemblies.[22] The harm would be particularly to the ability to raise funds, although there is obviously a strong public interest in how governments both raise and spend monies. You may need to consider if section 28 also applies when considering this exemption.

If you want to apply the economy exemption, you need to focus on the following points:

- The information in these areas is more likely to be time sensitive and it is less likely that the exemption will apply after a financial transaction than before it, unless the transaction is fairly regular.
- Public authorities that rely on their fees or other income in order

to operate can consider use of this exemption as well as section 43.
- The public interest will be tilted towards release, so you will need to show that the harm that would be caused by the release of the information definitely outweighs the public interest.
- However, you can take into account relations with local businesses and the potential harm to those relations.
- You can and should include any arguments relating to the effect on financial and other markets but will have to be able to demonstrate harm, which could be difficult to show concretely. This is an exemption where checking the decision notices relating to section 29 would help if you need to strengthen an argument.

Section 30 (FoIA)/section 34 (FoISA), Investigations and proceedings conducted by a [Scottish] public authority

If you do not have a duty or powers to investigate, you cannot use these exemptions. They can be used only by public authorities with a duty or powers to investigate whether someone should be prosecuted for an offence or proceedings that a public authority has the power to conduct. This obviously covers the police and regulators but will also cover other public authorities with investigative duties, like trading standards for local authorities and Fatal Accident Inquiries in Scotland.[23] I recommend reading paragraphs 7–9 of the SIC briefing on this section if you are new to Scotland and want an overview of how crime is prosecuted in Scotland. While both Acts cover information relating to the investigations and confidential sources, the FoISA covers Fatal Accident Inquiries as a separate section, 34(2). This section allows any Scottish public authority to exempt information relating to sudden or suspicious deaths even if it does not have a duty to investigate them.

For information to be exempt it must relate to investigations where there was an intent to charge someone. Information up to the time of being charged and beyond is exempt. The individual charged does not need to be found guilty, nor does the investigation have to lead to a court case.

Confidential sources information is also covered by this exemption, although it does not necessarily have to do with a particular case. Procedures for dealing with confidential sources would also be covered by this exemption. This part of sections 30/34 interacts quite closely with sections 31/35. For information from confidential sources to be exempt, it has to relate to the relationship between the public authority and the confidential source; that is, it has to be about the confidential source itself rather than the information it provides, which is more likely to be covered by sections 31/35.

In Scotland, any public authority can use this exemption for information relating to Fatal Accident Inquiries.

If you want to use this exemption, you must think about the following points:

- You do not have to reach the stage of prosecution in a court or via proceedings for these exemptions to apply. Pre-investigative work that could lead to a decision to prosecute is also covered.
- If you have information relating to your relationship with a confidential source, use these exemptions. If it is about the information they provide, use sections 31/35.

Section 31 (FoIA)/section 35 (FoISA), Law enforcement

These are the exemptions that can be potentially claimed by any public authority, so if you cannot apply section 30/34, look to see if there are any provisions in this section that apply. Section 31 is reproduced in full below, because there are many potential categories that can apply. This is from the FoIA, with any differences to the FoISA noted. This section is the only one reproduced in full, as it is the largest and covers prejudice to:

(1)(a) the prevention or detection of crime,
(b) the apprehension or prosecution of offenders,
(c) the administration of justice,
(d) the assessment or collection of any tax or duty or of any imposition of a similar nature,
(e) the operation of the immigration controls,
(f) the maintenance of security and good order in prisons or in other institutions where persons are lawfully detained,
(g) the exercise by any public authority of its functions for any of the purposes specified in subsection (2), [The FoISA includes

(within the meaning of the Freedom of Information Act 2000 (c.36)) or Scottish public authority' after any public authority.]

(h) any civil proceedings which are brought by or on behalf of a public authority and arise out of an investigation conducted, for any of the purposes specified in subsection (2), by or on behalf of the authority by virtue of Her Majesty's prerogative or by virtue of powers conferred by or under an enactment, [FoISA text is different but conveys the same meaning] or

(i) any inquiry held under the Fatal Accidents and Sudden Deaths Inquiries (Scotland) Act 1976 to the extent that the inquiry arises out of an investigation conducted, for any of the purposes specified in subsection (2), by or on behalf of the authority by virtue of Her Majesty's prerogative or by virtue of powers conferred by or under an enactment. [Not included in FoISA, which covers this in Section 34(2).]

(2) The purposes referred to in subsection (1)(g) to (i) are— [FoISA text uses 'to ascertain' for each subsection]

(a) the purpose of ascertaining whether any person has failed to comply with the law,

(b) the purpose of ascertaining whether any person is responsible for any conduct which is improper,

(c) the purpose of ascertaining whether circumstances which would justify regulatory action in pursuance of any enactment exist or may arise,

(d) the purpose of ascertaining a person's fitness or competence in relation to the management of bodies corporate or in relation to any profession or other activity which he is, or seeks to become, authorised to carry on,

(e) the purpose of ascertaining the cause of an accident,

(f) the purpose of protecting charities against misconduct or mismanagement (whether by trustees or other persons) in their administration,

(g) the purpose of protecting the property of charities from loss or misapplication,

(h) the purpose of recovering the property of charities,

(i) the purpose of securing the health, safety and welfare of persons at work, and

(j) the purpose of protecting persons other than persons at work against risk to health or safety arising out of or in connection with the actions of persons at work.

Law enforcement is considered to be quite broad in its application and does not just mean criminal activity. It includes complying with professional codes, protection of charities and health and safety at work, so potentially can be used by all public authorities.

This is both a prejudice test and a public interest test exemption. As always, the higher the likelihood of harm, the more likely the use of this exemption would pass the prejudice test. The public interest in being able to enforce the law will usually be high, but you will still have to consider arguments for release in the public interest.

When using this exemption, more specific advice is the following:

- You can consider use of the exemption where a picture could be built up of how and where investigations are occurring which would allow someone to pinpoint the weaknesses in the investigation (the Mosaic effect).
- Procedures are covered by 31/35(1)(a) if they would help to identify how to evade investigations.
- Information held by public authorities that cannot use section 30/34, but which would be used in an investigation carried out by public authorities that can, could be covered by 31/35(1)(b).
- Any information which on release would harm the ability of courts, tribunals and other judicial bodies to function and/or make it hard for an individual to receive a fair hearing is covered by section 31/35(1)(c).
- Section 31/35(1)(d) is engaged where release of information would stop tax from being collected or help tax evasion.
- Any information relating to immigration controls, including release of work permits or visas, is covered by section 31/35(1)(e).
- The harm in section 31/35(1)(f) extends to prisons, young offender institutes, secure hospitals and training centres, local authority secure units and immigration detention and removal centres.[24] The harm needs to relate to both the internal and external security of the unit.
- For the exemptions in section 31/35(2), you have to show that the

information relates to an attempt to ascertain, or find out, for example, the cause of an accident. You also have to be in the position to use that information for an investigation to prosecute an offender or revoke licences or set fines.[25]

- A public authority that is set up to enforce a code of conduct would use 31/35(2)(b), while regulators could use 31/35(2)(c) for information where release would harm their ability to carry out their regulatory functions. Section 31/35(2)(d) looks at whether information about fitness to practice is exempt.

Section 32 (FoIA)/section 37 (FoISA), Court records, etc.

Courts, tribunals and any other such legal bodies are outside the scope of the FoIA. So this exemption will cover only records that have been filed with or served on a public authority, or placed with an inquiry or arbitration service. If the information is held in records not in those circumstances, e.g. a human resources file versus the bundle going to an Employment Tribunal, the former cannot be covered by this exemption.

If you want to use this exemption you need to consider the following points:

- Firstly, you are very unlikely to ever use this exemption, unless you have a bundle of documents prepared for a court case and the information is not held anywhere else in the public authority.
- However, even if the case is concluded, you will be able to use the exemption, provided that it meets the condition above.

Section 33 (FoIA)/section 40 (FoISA), Audit functions

This is one exemption where the two Acts are different. Section 33 in the FoIA is available only to public authorities that have an audit function. If a public authority does not carry out audits on other public authorities, it cannot use this exemption. The FoISA allows other public authorities to use section 40, although only if release of the information would harm the work of a public authority with audit functions. Neither exemption covers internal audits or audits of private bodies. The focus is on the harm to the exercise of the auditor's functions on auditing another public authority's accounts or how that public authority has used the resources available to it.

If you are an auditing public authority, or in Scotland hold information relating to the work of an auditing public authority, you will need to think about the following points:

- You will likely know if you are a public authority that can use section 33, but it covers bodies with an inspectorate role as well, like Ofsted and HM Inspectorate of Prisons.
- If you are a Scottish public authority and release of the information could harm a public authority like the ones listed above, you can consider using section 40.
- Timeliness can affect the level of harm, so if release of an early version of a report could harm the audit, it could be exempted.

Section 34, Parliamentary privilege

Another exemption with a definite focus on particular public authorities, this covers unpublished information held within the House of Commons or House of Lords, the release of which would infringe on parliamentary privilege. There is no FoISA equivalent. This can be used only by Parliament.

Should you need to apply this exemption, keep in mind the following points:

- Parliamentary privilege is not defined in the Act but is understood to relate to how the House of Commons and House of Lords govern themselves without interference by the Crown or other outside bodies.
- The focus is on information relating to parliamentary proceedings, that is, the work of Parliament.

Section 35 (FoIA)/section 29 (FoISA), Formulation of government/Scottish administration policy

Both of these exemptions use more or less the same text and cover four classes of information that can be exempted. The public interest test applies. The first, 35/29(1)(a), relates to formulation of government policy, for which the public interest test will focus on how current the formulation is. The second, 35/29(1)(b), relates to communications between ministers, with an emphasis on maintaining collective responsibility. The third, 35/29(1)(c), relates to legal advice provided by the Law Officers and decisions to request it. The fourth, 35/29(1)(d), covers the operation of ministerial private offices.

Only central government departments and the Welsh Assembly plus some Northern Irish public bodies can use section 35. Other public authorities can consider section 36 (discussed below).

This is a fairly well tested exemption, so it is worth looking at the ICO decisions in this area. However, if you plan on using it, you will need to bear in mind the following:

- how you will apply the public interest test, as you need to carry this out even though this exemption is class based;
- at what point statistical information is in a process, as it cannot be covered by 35(1)(a) once a decision has been made;
- to apply 35/29(1)(a), the information must relate to policy, not operational decisions. It must also relate to the formulation rather than application of policy, although where policy review fits in can be difficult to determine;
- when applying 35/29(1)(b), the minister has to be involved in the communication. Information that summarises a minister's communication by another individual does not engage the exemption;
- section 35/29(1)(c) can be used only for information provided by or requested from the Attorney General, Solicitor General and their equivalents for the devolved assemblies, as these are the Law Officers. Other legal advice is not covered by this exemption, but will likely be covered by section 42/36(1);
- it is likely you can use section 42/36(1) as well as section 35/29(1)(c) for the same legal advice from the Law Officers. However, this section covers a wider range of information, as it can include discussions on whether to approach the Law Officers for advice and precis of the advice, as well as the legal opinion itself. However, the public interest test has to focus on the effect on government decision-making processes;[26]
- the operation and administration of a minister's office is covered

by section 35/29(1)(d). The ICO guidance states: 'it is limited to information about routine administrative and management processes, the allocation of responsibilities, internal decisions about ministerial priorities and similar issues'.[27] It does not cover information created in carrying out ministerial duties or a minister's private life. The latter would be covered by section 40/38.

Section 36, Prejudice to the effective conduct of public affairs

This exemption is available for public authorities that cannot use section 35. In a way, it acts as a catch-all exemption, in that it covers any harm to collective responsibility, free and frank exchange of advice and the effective conduct of public affairs in general. As such, it covers a multitude of situations. For example, universities have been able to use this exemption when students have requested examination solutions before the exams have been held.

The most difficult part of using this exemption is not that you have to pass both the prejudice and public interests tests, but the requirement to get an opinion from a qualified person. The qualified person is usually the chief executive officer (CEO) or their equivalent in a public authority, unless the information is statistical. They are expected to write an opinion on whether the exemption is engaged, and the ICO expects a public authority to produce this opinion if there is a complaint. If you have a CEO who is uninterested in the FoIA, or who would be unwilling to draft such an opinion, it can make this exemption very hard to use. If you do not have a qualified person at your public authority you cannot use this exemption without sign-off from the minister of a government department. If you are not sure which department to contact, contact the Ministry of Justice at informationrights@justice.gsi.gov.uk. Lack of co-operation from the qualified person becomes an issue if it is the only exemption that applies and the information should definitely be withheld. As such, you may need to make it as easy for them as possible. You can prepare a draft opinion and should be as firm as possible that the qualified person needs to see it and sign it off.

In order to use this exemption, you must cover the following points:

- The qualified person's opinion has to be reasonable. If the opinion contains an unlikely outcome, it is unlikely to be reasonable.
- The requirement of section 36(2)(a)(i) means that the harm has to be to collective responsibility, that is, a united front which may be covering differences of opinion.
- For section 36(2)(b), the qualified person's opinion has to relate to (i) advice or (ii) exchange of views for the purposes of deliberation and be clear which is engaged, or that both are.
- The harm for section 36(2)(b) is in whether advice and exchange of views would be harmed by release of the information. The harm has to be particular to the information in question, as generalised arguments of chilling effects are not acceptable to the ICO.
- Section 36(2)(c) is the exemption that covers any situation not covered by any other exemption, including the two subsections above.

Section 37 (FoIA)/section 41(FoISA), Communications with Her Majesty, etc. and Honours

This is another point at which the FoIA and the FoISA part company, due to amendments made to the FoIA in January 2011. The FoISA remains a qualified exemption which requires the public interest test and is time limited. The FoIA is now an absolute exemption for communications with the sovereign, heir to the throne and the second in line to the throne, with the latter two now specifically covered by section 37. It remains a qualified exemption for communications with other members of the Royal family and the Royal household as long as the sovereign, heir to the throne and second in line to the throne are not included. Both Acts include honours conferred by the Queen in this exemption.

You are likely to be fairly certain if this exemption applies, but should also consider the following points:

- With other members of the Royal family not being covered by the absolute exemption, seniority is less important than the nature of the information.
- Royal visits may also be covered by the exemptions relating to Security Bodies and National Security.

Section 38 (FoIA)/section 39(1) (FoISA), Health and safety

This exemption allows for the exemption of information that could harm the physical and mental health or safety of any individual. While the FoIA says 'endanger', this is considered to be the same as 'prejudice', so this exemption still focuses on harm. This does not have to be based on just one individual; for example, providing the locations of evacuation points could allow someone to target those points once an evacuation occurs, so those locations could be covered by section 38/39(1).

While it should be fairly obvious when this exemption applies, you will need to think about the following points:

- It may be easier to demonstrate physical rather than mental health, but where you think you have a good argument for mental health, you should make it.
- Be careful with 'neither confirm nor deny' with this exemption. You can undermine the use of this exemption by confirming that information exists.

Section 39 (FoIA)/section 39(2) (FoISA), Environmental information

Both these sections point to the relevant EIR, which will be discussed in Chapter 7. The test is that if the requested information falls within the definition of environmental information in the Regulations, the request falls under the Regulations rather than the Acts. However, in practice if the information is being provided, there is not much difference. It is only when the information is exempt that the exceptions in the Regulations should be considered instead ('exceptions' is the word the Regulations use for 'exemptions').

In summary, if it looks like environmental information, check the definition in the Regulations. If the information fits within the definition, apply the Regulations instead. The ICO/SIC will force you to reconsider if you have applied exemptions from the wrong piece of legislation.

Section 40 (FoIA)/section 38 (FoISA), Personal information

Like section 39/39(2), section 40/38 is where FoI meets another legal regime, in this case, the DPA up to 25 May 2018 and the GDPR and new DPA from that date onwards. However, this is not as straightforward as the DPA taking precedence, if only because the DPA is not like the EIR as just another way to request information. For both Acts, if someone is requesting their personal information, it is a straight swap to the subject access provisions of the DPA.[28] This is not the end of the request, as you are expected to immediately treat the request under section 7 of the DPA (see Chapter 5 for handling these requests). However, when third-party personal details are involved, things get messier and the two Acts part ways somewhat.

Both Acts have a multi-layered test for applying the exemption. For the FoIA, you must do the following:

1 Determine that the information requested is indeed personal; that is, that it satisfies the definition of personal data in DP legislation, and is data about a living individual who can be identified from that data or by a combination of that data and other information held by the data controller (see Chapters 4 and 5). If this personal data relates to the individual requesting it, section 7 of the DPA and/or the subject access rights of the General Data Protection Regulation (GDPR) come into play instead.
2 If the information is personal but relates to third parties, you have to consider first if releasing the information contravenes the data protection principles.[29] In practice, this will generally refer to the first data protection principle, fairness. This principle covers fairness, lawfulness and the need for a condition for processing under Article 6 for personal data generally and under Article 9 for special personal data as well. Ask yourself: is it fair to release the data? Would the data subject expect it? Would it be reasonable to release the data? For example, a senior staff member will have a higher expectation that their personal data may be released than a junior staff member, due to their difference in seniority and responsibility within the organization. Statistical information which hides the identity of the data subjects will be fairer to release than information which directly identifies an individual. Work expenses will be fairer to release than private financial information.
3 If the answer is yes, it would be fair, the ICO states that you must

then check for Schedule 2 and Schedule 3 conditions for processing. The GDPR means finding a lawful basis in Articles 6 and 9. Legal requirements would cover Schedule 2 and Article 6 obligations to respond to requests for information under the FoIA and FoISA. In this case, the processing is releasing the personal data for an FoI request. If you were to ask most public authorities, this is the part of the test which they have most likely never carried out. However, it is worth doing because, particularly for sensitive personal data, explicit consent to release may be your only option, which helps with the public interest test later on. If you cannot identify a condition for processing that would allow you to release the data, you should not release it. If the only available condition for processing is consent, you can consider how easy consent would be to obtain.

4 Another reason that you should consider is whether release would cause damage or distress to the data subject(s).[30] If it is likely to do so, you should not release the information. For example, you may be able to release a file held in an archive relating to a person who is retired, rather than information that covers someone starting their career, as the former is less likely to be damaged by release.

5 The last reason why you can exempt personal data is if it is exempt from release under the subject access provisions in the DPA.[31] If you have the ability not to release certain types of personal data to the data subject, you can refuse to release it to anyone else. This makes sense, because if someone cannot receive a copy of their own personal data, it would not be fair to release it to another person.

6 If you think it is fair and you have a Schedule 2 (and 3) condition for processing that allows you to release the information, then do so. If the personal data does fit one of the exemptions, you still have to consider if there is a legitimate reason to release it. If there is a particularly controversial issue, if the data relates to public finances or if the data would vindicate an individual, then consider release. Otherwise, it is exempt.

Section 38 of the FoISA is set out somewhat differently, although it retains the same split between information relating to the data subject and information relating to third parties. The tests above cover deciding what to do with personal data that could be exempt. However, this exemption also covers personal data held within a census[32] and the health records of the deceased.[33] Both of these are absolute exemptions, but time limited to 100 years. For the health records exemption to apply, they have to have been created by a health professional or at a health professional's behest.

If you have never used all the tests above to decide on whether to use this exemption, try them. You will be expected to show evidence that you have done so if a complaint goes to the ICO, and if you have used the tests thoroughly once or twice, you will be able to go through the steps a lot more quickly with further requests.

Section 41 (FoIA)/section 36(2) (FoISA), Information provided in confidence/Confidentiality

Confidentiality is an absolute exemption, but does require a prejudice test. The information has to have been provided to the public authority from a third party. This exemption cannot be used for information generated within the public authority. There are two main tests for this exemption to apply. The first is whether the information is confidential. The second test is whether it would be an actionable breach of confidence to supply it.

The test for confidentiality comes from common law[34] and is threefold. The information has to have the quality of confidence, that is, it cannot be in the public domain. It has to have been imparted with the expectation of confidentiality, so information that would soon be public knowledge is not covered. The last test is that release of the information would be harmful to the confider, unless the information relates to the confider's personal life.

Whether it is an actionable breach or not is determined by whether the confider would be able to take legal action against the public authority, should the information be released. You may not get as obvious an indication of this as 'We will sue you if you release this information' – which I got in a phone call for one request – but there has to be an ability to sue and a likelihood that legal action would take place.

To use this exemption, you have to have received the information from a third party. If you have information internally generated that requires confidentiality, section 40/38 will cover personal information and section 43/33 commercial-in-confidence information.

Section 42 (FoIA)/section 36(1) (FoISA), Legal professional privilege

Legal professional privilege (LPP) covers communications between a client and their lawyers. There are two kinds of LLP: litigation privilege and advice privilege. Litigation privilege covers information relating to an upcoming and/or ongoing court case. Advice privilege covers information relating to legal advice given when there is no litigation in view. The regulators will ask which you are applying, so be certain when deciding on this exemption which type of privilege applies.

To use this exemption, you must keep the following points in mind:

- The client in this case is not the public authority. It is the staff member(s) who is dealing with the legal professionals who are considered the client.
- This can become a time-bound exemption. If you were planning litigation but did not actually carry it out and several years have passed, it will be harder to apply this exemption and the ICO/SIC is more likely to require you to provide the information.

Section 43 (FoIA)/section 33 (FoISA), Commercial interests

Commercial interests is split into two types: trade secrets and commercial-in-confidence information. Trade secrets is an absolute exemption under the FoIA, but very hard to use. The information has to be unknown outside the organization that produced it and unlikely to be reproducible. If it would be relatively easy for another person to recreate the information from scratch themselves, it is not a trade secret. It is unlikely that information generated by a public authority will fit within the definition of a trade secret, but they may hold information like patents relating to third parties, which would be covered.

Commercial-in-confidence information is a qualified exemption and much broader in scope. However, the harm has to be to commercial, not financial, interests. Simply having to pay more or not saving money is not covered by this exemption, there has to be a harm to commercial competition. This makes it harder for most public authorities to use it for themselves, although if you can tie the harm to your ability to provide a (specific) service you will find it easier. Public authorities that have to fund themselves will find this an easier exemption to use than those fully funded by taxes and rates.

It is an easier exemption to use for contracted services, although the public interest test is important for this exemption, as there is a strong interest in the public getting value for money. However, specific prices and rates may be covered by this exemption if it would allow a competitor to undercut the contractor and if the contractor uses different prices and rates for the public sector as compared to the private sector.

It cannot be emphasised enough that the harm for commercial-in-confidence information is to commercial, not financial, interests. It has to harm the ability of the public authority to provide specific services or of a business to compete with other businesses. 'It will cost the public authority funds' in a general sense will not work with the ICO/SIC.

Section 44 (FoIA)/section 26 (FoISA), Prohibitions on disclosure

You will probably already know if you can use the first test in this exemption, as it deals with statutory bars, that is, legislation that forbids you from releasing certain information. The example provided in the ICO guidance on section 44 relates to the census, as the Census Act 1920 makes it an offence to release information relating to the census.[35] If the legislation does not state outright that it would be an offence to release, you are unlikely to be able to rely on this exemption.

The other prohibitions relate to EU obligations, that is, EU Regulations, Directives, Treaties, etc. that forbid release of information and contempt of court, which would apply where a public authority had been forbidden by a court with regard to disclosure of particular information.

If you are uncertain if your public authority is subject to any statutory bars, it would be worth talking to your legal team or solicitors about what these might be. This is also the case for EU obligations. Where you can, it would be useful to have a flag for information where release could lead to contempt of court. The ability to apply a legal hold would be helpful.

Section 14, Vexatious and repeated requests

Repeated requests are fairly easy to identify and you can refuse to supply the information on the basis that you are already working on the request or have already provided it.

Vexatious requests are not necessarily hard to identify, but, unlike the applicant-blind focus of the rest of the Acts, this is one area where you can take the behaviour of a requester into account. However, it remains the case that the request is vexatious, not the individual, no matter how vexed that individual is making you or your colleagues feel. To a degree, vexatiousness is in the category of 'you can recognise it when you see it'. However, the tests for a request to be vexatious are: '(1) the burden (on the public authority and its staff); (2) the motive (of the requester); (3) the value or serious purpose (of the request) and (4) any harassment or distress (of and to staff)'.[36] As such, if the request creates a heavy burden for the public authority and its staff, and/or the motive behind the request is not simply to gain information, and/or the request has no serious purpose, and/or the staff who need to comply with the request are legitimately harassed or distressed by it, the more likely it is that the request is vexatious.

You may get a request so unreasonable that you recognise it as vexatious immediately. Or it may be the 30th related request you've received on a particular topic from the same person that week. Other requests are harder to identify, and, particularly if there is a serious purpose, consider treating the request on its merits. For example, if someone has a legitimate complaint about the public authority, requesting information that helps them through the complaints process is unlikely to be vexatious. However, if they keep requesting information after the resolution of their complaint or asking for information in different ways which you have already provided, or which you have informed them does not exist, you can then judge the request as vexatious.

Also, remember that once you have provided the refusal notice, section 17(6) of the FoIA and section 16(5) of the FoISA allow you to not respond to any further requests which you have already refused as vexatious or repeated.

Writing the refusal notice

Whenever you write a refusal notice, you have to keep in mind that this is possibly going to the ICO/SIC and therefore include what they would expect to see regarding the use of particular exemptions. You also do not want to be so technical in your language that the requester cannot understand it. So remember the following points:

- Be clear about what exemptions are being used and what information they cover.
- Use the word 'harm' rather than 'prejudice' when conducting the prejudice test. This is an easier test than the public interest test. Either there will be or there is a possibility of harm, or there will not be.
- Include arguments for release in the public interest.

Doing a proper but easy-to-follow public interest test is not easy. You do have to consider what the public interest is in releasing as well as in exempting the information and show that you have actually considered both. Sometimes it can be easy to identify, for example, a live issue where release of the information could help to illuminate that what happened could mean that the balance lies in release of the information. However, sometimes it will be hard to identify a specific reason for release other than general transparency.

It can also be difficult to identify arguments as to why the public interest lies in exempting the information. It can be harder to get colleagues to provide arguments relating to public interest than arguments relating to use of the exemption itself. So, continue to press your colleagues until you think that you have enough information to make a decent public interest test argument.

Good and bad examples can be found on the What Do They Know website.[37]

Dealing with complaints and follow-up requests

Not everyone will be happy with the response you have sent them. Sometimes you will receive a follow-up requesting clarification on a particular point, which will generally be easy to deal with. Sometimes it will be in the form of a brand new request, in which case you repeat the process of handling an FoI request. Other times it will be a request for internal review, which is the first step in the FoI complaints process. This can be followed by a complaint to the ICO/SIC. The next step after that is the Information Tribunal, which provides case law (see below). After that, complaints can be taken through the courts up to the Supreme Court. However, it is unlikely that you will go further than the ICO/SIC.

What is case law and why is it important?

Case law is produced through court judgments. It is important because it sets precedent. That is, if a judgment says that an exemption should be applied in a certain way, you must follow that reasoning from then on until a higher court says otherwise. ICO/SIC decisions do not set precedent, although it is generally wise to follow what they say. Information Tribunal judgments, however, do set precedent, and so they do need to be followed unless a higher court judgment exists.

Internal review

The FoISA in section 21 sets out that an internal review should be carried out and that it should take 20 working days to complete. The FoIA does not have a specific section. The section 45 Code of Practice refers to internal reviews, although without a time scale. However, the ICO has made it clear that 20 working days is a reasonable period of time.

The internal review should be carried out by someone who has not been involved in the previous response. The internal reviewer should be at least equal in grade to the staff member who responded, if not more senior. Always have at least one back-up internal reviewer, if not two – people go on holiday and the deadlines still have to be met.

The internal reviewer will need to talk to the original responder to find out more detail on exemptions used and how the public interest and prejudice tests were applied. They can decide that the exemptions were originally misapplied and uphold the complaint, or that some of the information that was withheld could be released. They can also decide if other exemptions should be brought into play.

All internal review responses should direct the requester to the ICO/SIC.

Complaints to the ICO/SIC

Requesters can complain to the ICO/SIC if they are unhappy with the response or if they did not receive a response either to the original request or to a request for internal review. The regulator will then contact the public authority asking for details relating to the public authority's decisions and evidence of how it came to them.

While you should have included the basic arguments in the response and the internal review, you will have to provide more detail at this level. If there are specific questions asked, you will need to answer them. You do not get a huge amount of time to respond, but, like communications with the requester, let the regulator know if you are going to have problems meeting their deadline and when you should be able to respond to them.

At this point you are free to seek legal advice if you have not already done so. You will also need to get any certificates ready for information that cannot be shared with the regulator. In your response to the complaint you should state if any information should be kept confidential by the regulator.

You may find that there is some back and forth once you have made your initial response to the regulator. The questions will get more specific as the regulator probes into why you have applied a particular exemption. A few months later you will get the decision notice. If this is not agreeable to either side, you can appeal to the Information Tribunal for UK public authorities, or the Inner House of the Court of Sessions for Scottish public authorities.

Tribunals and the courts

The requester and/or the public authority can appeal a decision notice. The appeal needs to be lodged in the UK with the Information Tribunal within 28 days of the decision notice being sent out or with the Inner House of the Court of Sessions within 42 days for decisions relating to Scottish public authorities. Technically, it is the regulator whose decision is being appealed, but if a public authority feels strongly enough about representing its views in court, it can ask to be joined.

Anonymous, County Council says:

> Who the appellant is will dictate to a large extent the amount of administrative work required for an appeal to the Tribunal; if the authority is appealing an ICO decision, more of the administrative burden will fall on that authority, e.g. creating bundles (it is still very much a paper process). It follows that cost cannot be ignored when deciding whether to appeal a decision notice that has gone against an authority.
>
> On the other side, if it is the applicant that is appealing the ICO decision notice an authority has to decide whether to seek to be joined to the appeal. Some negotiation can be a good idea – if both parties can come to an agreement on what extra could be disclosed, everyone (especially the Tribunal!) will be happy at the saving to the public purse (although negotiating at the ICO investigation stage is probably a better idea still). If an authority is party to an appeal it is advisable to instruct a counsel from a law firm experienced in information law. The practicalities of any instruction would normally be carried out by the internal legal service, and your counsel will normally follow the line you set out, although they will of course advise on its merits/alternatives. Depending on the appeal, a lot of work can be required in drafting a submission, and normally to time scales set out in any directions.
>
> It is obviously cheaper (free) to not be joined, but more risky, in that a Tribunal can decide only on the basis of what information is before it; without being joined, a public authority will be in no position to challenge any inaccurate submissions made by an appellant. Most authorities would probably be satisfied with a paper hearing, but often appellants want an oral hearing (which means more cost); a public authority might not have to attend, but not doing so is again a risk. Most of the running of an authority's case at an oral hearing will be undertaken by counsel, and the FoI Officer will be more seen than heard (they may pass notes to the counsel if appropriate), although it is not impossible that a FoI Officer will be asked for their input directly, as almost certainly they will have more direct knowledge of a case than anyone else. What is presented at an oral hearing should go beyond what is in the submissions, and it might be worth considering whether to call any witnesses (although they could, of course, be cross-examined).

At the hearings I have attended, the Tribunal does tend to make allowances for members of the public who are representing themselves; I would just say that at one of our hearings the member of the public concerned had far more experience in such hearings than we did! Hearings are open to the public, so I would advise any FoI Officer to attend one to get the feel for them (I attended two as an observer before having to be part of one myself, and felt that this was an invaluable experience). Contact the Tribunal Service to let them know if you plan to attend. Hearings are listed here: https://www.gov.uk/government/ publications/ information-rights-register-of-tribunal-cases.

Preparing for a hearing as an FoI officer is very time consuming, as there will be lots of information to collate, review, thoughts to be put on paper, notes on the appellant's position to be made, questions from counsel to be answered – it could very easily take a solid week on the one case. My own personal view is that, due to the potential cost in terms of money and time, you have to think very seriously before committing to an appeal/being joined to an appeal; It might be that you simply accept a decision even though you disagree with it. The impact of following the decision notice (e.g. disclosing information that you think should be exempt) will not always be enough to warrant challenging it.

If given leave on a point of law for FoIA requests, either the requester or the public authority can continue to appeal through court system to the Supreme Court.

Publication schemes and disclosure logs

Both Acts require public authorities to produce a publication scheme, which lists and, if it is on a website, links to the information you regularly publish. Judging by the requests received, requesters do not look to see what is available before making a request. So, follow the model publication schemes provided by the regulators because you are required to, but concentrate your resources on responding to requests.

While they are not a requirement, disclosure logs are recommended for making available information to the general public after a request. Whether or not you do this depends on the level of resources available to your public authority, as you do have to ensure that personal data relating to requesters is redacted before publication. As for the publication scheme, the evidence is equivocal as to whether or not they actually head off requests.

In spite of my general scepticism about the publication of FoI responses, it can be useful in terms of making use of the sections 21/25 and 22/27 exemptions. It is easier to provide a link to what is already on your website than to produce the information afresh, and it is useful to know, for example, that statistics will be updated yearly, so next year's will be available to requesters at some point.

Conclusion

Now that you have finished this chapter, you should know:

- what the exemptions are for both the FoIA and FoISA;
- how to apply the exemptions;
- how to perform a public interest test;
- how to determine whether harm will occur for the prejudice test exemptions;
- how to determine if a request breaches the cost limit;
- how to determine if a request is vexatious;
- how to handle complaints;
- how to cover the publication scheme requirements.

For guidance on how to recognise and process a request, see Chapter 2.

For the basics of processing requests for environmental information, see Chapter 2.

See Chapter 7 for advice on how to recognise environmental-related information and the exceptions related to providing it.

4

Data protection: principles and main features

Introduction

Unlike Freedom of Information and the Environment Information Regulations, data protection is not just a straightforward request for information. It includes requests for personal information, but is also meant to govern how personal data is collected, used, managed and disposed of by organizations.

On 25 May 2018, the General Data Protection Regulation (GDPR) came into force within the EU member states. The Regulation applies in the UK, through the Data Protection Act (DPA) 2018, which also incorporates how to manage personal data relating to law enforcement and intelligence services.

In many ways, the GDPR builds on the Data Protection legislation produced under the previous Directive.

Above all, keep in mind: the main point of data protection is to let individuals know what you are doing with their personal information. Transparency is the key.

Data Protection has a lot of different aspects, so has been divided into three chapters. If you are the official Data Protection Officer (DPO) or supporting that role, you will need to be able to respond on all of the following:

- Chapter 4 covers the basics: the principles, including data breaches, definitions, lawful basis for processing, special

categories data and the difference between data controllers and data processors.
- Chapter 5 covers how to respond to requests relating to personal data, including subject access, deletion, portability, marketing and automated processing. In other words, it covers requests from individuals about their data.
- Chapter 6 covers internal enquiries about data protection that you are likely to receive from colleagues. It includes guidance on privacy notices, data protection impact assessments and how to handle the sorts of questions you are likely to receive relating to personal data.

First, though, is an explanation of the differences between the former Directive that led to the 1998 DPA and Regulations.

Regulations and Directives

The GDPR is a Regulation, whereas the EU law it replaces was a Directive. What is the difference?

A Directive is intended to be translated by the EU member states into individual legislation within those states. So the EU Directive (95/46/EC) was the precursor to the 1998 DPA in the UK and similar legislation in the other EU member states. This meant that each piece of legislation based on the Directive had its own individual quirks.

A Regulation is a law that applies across the EU member states without needing to be translated into national law. The intention was to help cross-border flows of data within the EU and to ensure that data subject rights were the same. However, there are derogations within the GDPR which enable member states to set their own laws in those areas, for example, regarding exemptions.

There is also a Directive for personal data relating to law enforcement (LED), which requires national law. It was decided to make this outside the scope of the GDPR as there was less agreement in this area amongst member states. Legislation needed to be produced by 6 May 2018. This has been incorporated into the DPA 2018.

EU legislation includes recitals (descriptive text setting out the reason for the articles) and the articles themselves, which stipulate the requirements of the Regulation and Directives. Generally, you will be following the requirements of the articles, but it is worth looking at the recitals as well, as they will help to further your understanding of what the articles require. For example, health is included as one of the special categories of data in Article 9(1). But a wider definition of health is included in Recital 54, to help determine if the personal data you are processing fits within that category.

So, what is the position in the UK? The DPA 2018 brings together the GDPR in part 2, the LED in part 3 and covers intelligence services processing in part 4. The Information Commissioner's powers are covered in part 5 and enforcement, including penalties in part 6. There are 18 Schedules which cover the exemptions available, amongst other things. Many of the exemptions from the previous DPA have been ported over, even if they are not listed in the GDPR. The intent of the new Act is to ensure adequacy once the UK has left the European Union. It remains to be seen if that will be the case.

Other EU countries will also be producing their own Data Protection legislation to cover the derogations and their own local responses to these. For example, Germany produced its Bundesdatenschutzgesetz in 2017 to replace their previous DPA.

Data protection main features

Up to 25 May 2018, your organization should already have been:

- managing personal data with regards to the data protection principles;
- only processing personal data when a condition for processing could be identified;
- managing requests for their own personal information from data subjects (subject access requests);
- managing requests for changes to and deletions of personal data, where inaccurate;
- informing data subjects of any automated processing and allowing for their objections to this;
- registering with the ICO the types of personal data processed, the types of individuals involved and who the data is shared with.

You still have to do all these things under the GDPR. However you also have to:

- manage requests for data portability and extended rights on data deletion;
- record what personal data you keep and make these records available on demand to the ICO and data subjects;
- appoint a DPO, depending on the size of your organization or the amount of personal data handled;
- report data breaches to the ICO within 72 hours of becoming aware of them;
- ensure that data processors are contractually obliged to process personal data legally;
- incorporate privacy by design into systems managing personal data, including the requirement to conduct a privacy impact assessment in certain conditions.

Compliance with the old DPA was a good basis for being compliant with the GDPR. In the UK, compliance with the new DPA should help compliance with the GDPR.

What is personal data?

So, what actually is personal data as defined by the GDPR? Personal data is defined as

> any information relating to an identified or identifiable natural person ('data subject'); an identifiable natural person is one who can be identified, directly or indirectly, in particular by reference to an identifier such as a name, an identification number, location data, an online identifier or to one or more factors specific to the physical, physiological, genetic, mental, economic, cultural or social identity of that natural person.

To break down parts of the definition:

- *identified or identifiable*: some personal data obviously identifies an individual, e.g. name, a photograph of their face. Other personal data can be used to identify an individual with a bit of work, e.g.

IP addresses, a post code that applies to a single dwelling;
- *natural person*: not an organization or business. GDPR applies to individual human beings only.

The list of possible identifiers is fairly broad in order to try to encompass all of the possible types of personal data that could relate to an individual. Genetic material is specifically mentioned for the first time. Name is also specifically mentioned, which renders the judgment in Durant moot: 'mere mention of a name' no longer applies, as now names are specifically personal data.

Definitions

The DPA 1998 was known as a very jargon-heavy document and the GDPR is no different. However, there are two main definitions that you will have to keep in mind regarding both:

- Data subject. The data subject is the natural person that the data is about or refers to. That's why requests for an individual's own information are known as subject access requests. While as a professional you will need to know what 'data subject' refers to, it may be better in guidance which you produce for your organization to refer to individuals, or specific client groups like students, patients, customers, etc. The goal of your guidance is to connect the rights of data subjects to the individuals whom your organization actually deals with. It should also help staff to identify where personal data is stored for the record-keeping requirements of the GDPR.
- Data controller. The data controller is the organization, public or private, one-person or multinational, on whose behalf the personal data is being processed. The idea of the data controller appears to confuse some people, who expect that it is a specific person within the organization. There is no such person, it is the organization as a whole which is the data controller. This is why it is the organization on which fines will be levied, the organization that will have to sign undertakings, etc. Your chief executive or main director may be the person who signs on the organization's behalf, but they are not the 'data controller'. Neither is the DPO.

Other definitions will be explained in either this chapter or the next two.

The data protection principles

The DPA had eight Data Protection principles. The GDPR has six, with two of the previous principles being turned into articles in their own right. The GDPR principles are below, where you will find an explanation of what each principle means, followed by how best to guide your staff to work by them.

Principle 1: fairness

Article 5(a) states that personal data will be 'processed lawfully, fairly and in a transparent manner in relation to individuals'.

Lawfully means in accordance with the GDPR and any supporting legislation, like the DPA 2018. Fairly is more general than that. It covers the expectations of data subjects regarding their data. You have to treat the data as you would wish yours to be treated, so it covers the need to let individuals know what you are doing with their data, to not use it in a way contrary to their interests and to not pass it on to other organizations or individuals without the knowledge of the data subject. Fairness and transparency support each other. It will be hard to say you are treating individuals fairly if you are not being transparent with them about what you are doing with their data. There are some exemptions, normally relating to national security, defence and processing relating to crime, where you do not have to notify data subjects that you are processing their data. But these should be used only where necessary.

What do staff need to do to comply?

Actions required by principle 1 to support transparency are:

- privacy notices and consent forms;
- data protection impact assessments;
- determining the legal basis for processing;
- maintaining records relating to personal data.

Principle 2: collection for specified purposes

Article 5(b) requires that personal data will be 'collected for specified, explicit and legitimate purposes and not further processed in a manner that is incompatible with those purposes; further processing for archiving purposes in the public interest, scientific or historical research purposes or statistical purposes shall not be considered to be incompatible with the initial purposes'.

This principle covers what you do with personal data when you first collect it and what is allowed if you want to use it for a different purpose. You have to have a specific purpose in mind for every piece of personal data that you want to collect. Your organization needs to determine what data it really needs in order to perform a task and what is only nice to have. You cannot collect data with the vague thought that you might need it some day. You cannot collect data that you cannot justify processing through one of the conditions for processing. It will be part of the record-keeping requirements of the GDPR to show that you are complying with this Article.

Once data is collected and used for a particular purpose, you cannot then use it for a completely different process. For example, if you have collected contact details for a particular event, you cannot then use this data for selling a product. However, you may be able to use them to notify the individuals concerned of a similar event if they have not indicated that they want no further contact from you.

The exceptions to this are mentioned in the Article. You can deposit personal data in an archive or reuse it for scientific and historical research purposes or for the purpose of creating statistics. For these activities, you will not breach the second principle.

What do staff need to do to comply?

Actions required by principle 2 are:

- thinking about what personal data is really needed;
- creating privacy notices/consent forms that request only the data needed;
- using the data collected for only that specific purpose unless:
  — it has historic, archival, research value;

– you have obtained consent from the data subject to use it for another purpose.

Principle 3: adequacy

Article 5(c) requires that all personal data collected are 'adequate, relevant and limited to what is necessary in relation to the purposes for which they are processed'. This supports the second principle. You can process enough of the personal data that you need to in order to perform the task that you need to undertake. The data needs to be relevant for that task and only include the personal data which you really need to perform it.

What do staff need to do to comply?

Actions required by principle 3 are similar to principle 2 and are:

- thinking about what personal data is really needed;
- creating privacy notices/consent forms that contain only the data needed.

Principle 4: accuracy

Article 5(d) requires that personal data are 'accurate and, where necessary, kept up to date; every reasonable step must be taken to ensure that personal data that are inaccurate, having regard to the purposes for which they are processed, are erased or rectified without delay'.

The accuracy principle should help both the individual whom the data is about and your organization to ensure that the personal data you are processing is the right personal data. This will mean ensuring that changes to personal circumstances – e.g. legitimate name changes, addresses, bank details – can also trigger changes in the personal data you hold on individuals. However, 'where necessary, kept up to date' allows for personal data which is a snapshot of a particular time to be kept as well. This principle ties into the rights of erasure and rectification given to data subjects by the GDPR.

What do staff need to do to comply?

Actions required by principle 4 are:

- responding in a timely fashion to requests to correct personal data. This can mean:
  - updating the personal data in the way requested by the data subject, e.g. 'my surname is spelt Maguire not McGuire';
  - adding a note to the data or file which includes the data subject's corrections, e.g. when a report has been given by a third party that the data subject objects to but which you cannot judge is right or wrong;
  - providing the data subject with a reason as to why the data cannot be updated, e.g. the personal data is a snapshot in time and reflects what was happening at the point the personal data was captured;
- where necessary, cleansing data. This could be done by:
  - providing a web portal where data subjects can check the data held on them and either update it themselves or report where changes are necessary, like address changes;
  - sending out by letter or e-mail the data held and asking data subjects to update it and send it back.

Principle 5: kept no longer than necessary

Article 5(e) requires that personal data are:

> kept in a form which permits identification of data subjects for no longer than is necessary for the purposes for which the personal data are processed; personal data may be stored for longer periods insofar as the personal data will be processed solely for archiving purposes in the public interest, scientific or historical research purposes or statistical purposes subject to implementation of the appropriate technical and organizational measures required by the GDPR in order to safeguard the rights and freedoms of individuals.

Like the second principle, principle 5 allows for personal data to be kept indefinitely if it will be used for archival, research or statistical purposes. However, personal data not being kept for these purposes must be destroyed when it is no longer necessary for a particular purpose. This applies while the data identifies an individual; anonymised data is not covered by the GDPR, so is outside the scope of the Regulation. One way, then, to keep data or to prepare it for long term use is to anonymise it.

Personal data kept indefinitely for archival, research or statistical purposes is still subject to security requirements and the rights of data subjects. If you keep it, you will still have to provide it via a subject access request, rectify it and erase it, unless you can justify not doing so.

What do staff need to do to comply?

Actions required by principle 5 are:

- determining the time period for which the data should be kept and adding this to the information asset register or whatever you are using for personal data record keeping (see the accountability principle section below);
- determining the trigger for that time period, e.g. when the staff member leaves, at the end of the calendar year, x years after the event occurs, etc.;
- applying both the time period and the trigger where necessary.

Principle 6: kept secure

Article 5(f) requires that personal data are 'processed in a manner that ensures appropriate security of the personal data, including protection against unauthorised or unlawful processing and against accidental loss, destruction or damage, using appropriate technical or organizational measures'.

Assuming that you do not come from an information security background, you still need to know enough about information security in order to help your organization comply with this particular principle. If you do not have a working knowledge of encryption, you need to develop one. This principle requires you to work with your organization's information security team, as they will have the technical knowledge to help protect personal data as well as being the only other people at your organization likely to have a good knowledge of data protection law. By working with your information security colleagues, you can develop the policies, procedures and guidance to help staff know:

- how to identify the information they need to protect via a security classification code, for example, 'confidential' or 'highly confidential'. Staff are also likely to need training to help use it;
- how to protect the data that has been identified as needing protection, for example by using encryption and other tools like secure online file transfer services;
- how to handle data security breaches. You will need to focus on what personal data is affected by the breach and, if you are the official DPO for your organization, be the official conduit for any communications and concerns which the affected data subjects will have. Your information security colleagues will be the ones dealing with the systems themselves, checking for flaws and the ways in which the systems can be fixed to ensure that the same breach does not occur again. This is explained in more detail below.

Article 32 includes some of the techniques and tests required to show that you are keeping to this principle, including use of pseudonymisation and encryption and 'regularly testing, assessing and evaluating the effectiveness of technical and organizational measures for ensuring the security of the processing'.[1]

What do staff need to do to comply?

Actions required by principle 6 are:

- to inform you or your information security colleagues when a breach occurs;
- to follow your organization's mandated information security practices regarding encryption, managing passwords and security classifications.

Managing data breaches

The GDPR has strengthened the requirement to report security data breaches to the relevant supervisory authority. In the UK, this is the ICO. Reports must be made within 72 hours of your organization becoming aware of a breach. So you do not need to be hyper-aware of everything going on with data, but do have to be in a position to report to the ICO or whichever supervising authority you have to report to.

The Article 29 Working Party guidance covers what a data breach is, when you become aware of it and communicating to both the data subjects and the ICO.

Data breaches are not necessarily just someone unauthorised getting access to the data. It also includes a loss of data that means you can no longer access it yourself. However, as you also have to consider the risk in the breach before notifying the ICO, it could be that the loss of the only copy of personal data on an encrypted device may not need notification.

You become aware of the data breach when you have 'a reasonable degree of certainty that a security incident has occurred that has led to personal data being compromised'.[2] So, if someone tells you they have received the personal data of another individual, you are aware when you receive their report. It may take longer to realise that a breach has occurred if it is due to an error with the code in an online system.

While you need to notify the ICO within 72 hours, you should provide a summary of what you know at that point and then follow up with a more detailed report once you have investigated further. The ICO has an online form to fill in for reporting a data breach, and which sets out the information it expects to receive.

You do not necessarily have to tell data subjects about a breach, but should do so where the risk to those individuals is high, e.g. if birth date or national insurance numbers or similar uniquely identifying information has been released. It can be better to let them know anyway, to show that you are being transparent and to let them know how you are mitigating the breach.

If you identify certain actions that will mitigate the breach, particularly if these will stop further breaches, communicate them to the ICO. It can either approve or suggest alternatives. Then carry out these mitigating actions. The ICO will be back to ensure that you have done so, particularly if it issued an enforcement notice or signed an undertaking with you on account of the breach.

The accountability principle

This is not a principle in its own right, but has been introduced in the GDPR. It requires that a data controller can be accountable to data subjects. In practice, this means being transparent about what personal data you are collecting and what you are doing with it.

Previous principles turned articles

Previous principles that are now articles (or a group of articles) in their own right relate to data subject rights (previously data protection principle 6) and transfers outside the EU (previously data protection principle 8). These have been expanded, with the rights of data subjects in both areas strengthened.

Kept in accordance with the data subjects rights

This used to be principle 6 in the DPA. However, the GDPR transforms this into a suite of rights for data subjects covered by:

- information to be provided where personal data are collected from the data subject (Article 13);
- information to be provided where personal data are not obtained from the data subject (Article 14);
- right of access by the data subject (Article 15);
- right to rectification (Article 16);
- right to erasure ('right to be forgotten') (Article 17);
- right to restriction of processing (Article 18);
- right to data probability (Article 20);
- right to object to processing (Article 21);
- rights relating to automated processing and profiling (Article 22).

The Article 13 and 14 obligations are covered in Chapter 6, Data protection enquiries. The other rights are discussed in Chapter 5, Data protection requests.

Transfers outside the EU

Transfers outside the EU now get their own chapter – Chapter V, covering Articles 44 to 50, having been expanded from a single principle. The conditions for transfers are discussed in Chapter 6, Data protection enquiries.

Conditions for processing/lawfulness of processing

In the DPA the conditions under which you could process personal data were in Schedule 2 for all personal data and Schedule 3 for sensitive personal data. You needed both a Schedule 2 and a Schedule 3 condition for processing sensitive personal data, and will need an Article 6 and Article 9 lawful basis for special categories personal data. The conditions for sensitive personal data, now called special categories data, are discussed in the next section.

Consent

There are many similarities between the old Schedule 2 conditions and the legal processing listed in Article 6. Consent is still the first condition (Article 6(a)), although expanded within Article 6 to say that it has to be for one or more specific purposes, and also via Articles 7 and 8. Article 7 lays out:

- how consent needs to be properly documented (Article 7(a));
- that consent cannot be hidden within a document but has to be clear to the data subject (Article 7(b));
- that consent can be withdrawn at any time, should be as easy to withdraw as to give, but withdrawal will not affect any processing done while the consent was given (Article 7(c));
- that consent in contracts needs to be handled carefully (Article 7(d)). It is worth considering if Article 6(b), which covers the performance of a contract or the steps necessary to entering a contract, is a better choice than consent. If you need personal data to carry out the terms of a contract or to set one up, consent is not the right condition because it can be withdrawn at any time.

Consent has to be freely given and unambiguous. However, consent is not the only condition for processing in the GDPR and most of the time will not be the best condition to use. The other articles below also allow for the processing of personal data without needing the express consent of the individuals concerned and you should consider if they apply before looking at consent.

Contract

Article 6(b) covers processing related to a contract entered into by a data subject or 'in order to take steps at the request of the data subject prior to entering into a contract'.[3] It is unlikely that determining if this condition should be used will be confusing. Either the processing will relate to a contract or entering into a contract with a data subject, or it will not.

Legal

Like Article 6(b), which is very similar to the Schedule 2 condition for contracts, Article 6(c) covers legal obligations. It is likely that any processing you do for tax purposes, for audit purposes or because of particular legislation will be covered by Article 6(c).

Vital interests of the data subject

Article 6(d) on first glance looks like the Schedule 2 condition relating to vital interests, but expands this from the data subject only to any other natural person. The ICO guidance on this condition restricts the use of this condition to life or death situations like road accidents.[4] However, the Recital 46 also includes processing relating to humanitarian purposes and emergencies, such as the spread of epidemics or processing required for managing natural or man-made disasters.

Public task

Articles 6(e) and 6(f) are where there is a real difference between the DPA and GDPR. Article 6(e) is covered in this subsection, and 6(f) in the next one. Only public authorities can use this lawful basis.

The Schedule 2 section 5 condition in the DPA listed several public bodies including the Houses of Parliament, the Crown, government departments and courts which could legitimately process personal data, with a catch-all in section 5(d) covering 'other functions of a public nature exercised in the public interest by any person'.[5] This is stripped down in Article 6(e) to 'the performance of a task carried out in the public interest or in the exercise of official authority vested in the controller'.

There has been discussion as to how far this covers public authorities and for what. The DPA 2018 sets out that any organizations that are considered public authorities for FoI purposes are also public authorities for the purpose of the GDPR. This offers some clarity. However, there is little clarification on what a 'task carried out in the public interest or in the exercise of official authority vested in the controller' will be. The second half of the definition appears to cover any legislative powers held by a public authority, which is relatively straightforward. Either you will have such powers or you will not. The first half could mean practically anything else a public authority does. Or does it?

The answer for some public authorities will be yes. It is likely that a local government organization will be processing personal data only due to its official authority or as a task in the public interest. However, some organizations, like universities, will be hybrid authorities. They will be considered to have public tasks like teaching and research which will be covered by Article 6(e). But other activities like fundraising will be covered by Article 6(f). If your organization is a public authority, you will need to consider whether your entire organization is considered to be carrying out public tasks or whether you have scope for legitimate interests. It may not become clear until we get some case law in this area.

Legitimate interests

Article 6(f) allows for the legitimate interests of the data controller, so it is similar to the legitimate interests in Schedule 2, section 6. However, Article 6(f) cannot be used by public authorities in the performance of their public tasks. Public authorities must use Article 6(e) to justify processing personal data, or one of the first four conditions for lawful processing when processing that sort of personal data.

Article 6(f) is worth looking at in full: 'processing is necessary for the purposes of the legitimate interests pursued by the controller or by a third party, except where such interests are overridden by the interests or fundamental rights and freedoms of the data subject which require protection of personal data, in particular where the data subject is a child'.[6] So, if you have a legitimate interest, you will still not be able to process the data if it could be said that the processing would be against the interests or fundamental rights and freedoms of data subjects. Recital 47 specifically states that marketing and protection against fraud are legitimate interests that would be covered by this article. Legitimate interests will cover collection of personal contact data, but you will still have to comply with the Privacy and Electronic Communications Regulations, depending on what sort of contact you want to make with individuals (see Chapter 8).

Special categories of personal data

Special categories of personal data is the equivalent to sensitive personal data in the DPA. While personal data relating to crime is now covered by a separate Directive, the other sensitive personal data are still special categories within Article 9. So this includes:

- racial or ethnic origin;
- political opinions;
- religious or philosophical beliefs;
- trade union membership;
- data relating to health;
- data relating to a natural person's sex life and sexual orientation. Whether this covers sex/gender is not defined by the GDPR.

Added to these are biometric and genetic data where these are used to identify a natural person. Biometric and genetic data are defined in Article 4 in sections 14 and 13, respectively.

Article 9 lists the specific lawful bases for processing special categories personal data.

General prohibition against processing the special categories

Article 9(1) prohibits the processing of these special categories of personal data. This does not apply if one of the conditions for processing in Article 9(2) applies. These are similar to the conditions for processing in Schedule 3 of the DPA.

Explicit consent

Article 9(2)(a) allows for the explicit consent of the data subject, unless this is prohibited by EU or member state law. The same requirements for explicit consent that held under the DPA 1998 are still needed for the GDPR. You have to be able to demonstrate that you have definitely asked for and obtained consent. When collecting demographic data, it is best practice to give individuals the chance to leave that part of a form blank or, if giving them a list of options, to include 'prefer not to say' or similar text.

Employment, social security and social protection

Article 9(2)(b) covers processing necessary for a data controller or data processor to comply with requirements relating to employment, social security and social protection law. Schedule 3 section 9 covered processing of racial data for equality purposes but did not cover other data covered by the Equalities Act. This article covers that data, so it is more useful to organizations.

Vital interest, unable to consent

Article 9(2)(c) covers processing in the vital interests of the data subject where they are incapable of providing consent. So it covers medical emergencies where the individuals are unconscious or incapable of consent due to impairment.

Processing by foundational or not-for-profit organizations

Article 9(2)(d) covers processing of personal data by foundational (this is 'not established' in the DPA) or not-for-profit organizations with a political, philosophical, religious or trade union aim. You are likely to be aware if you are in this category. Processing is restricted to members, former members or individuals in regular contact with the organization. This personal data cannot be released outside the organization without the consent of the data subjects.

Data subject made public

Article 9(2)(e) allows for processing of special categories of data made public by the data subject. So, if someone releases a photo of themselves from which their race or ethnicity could be determined, this article may allow for processing of that data. However, you do have to be careful, as you may determine special category data wrongly. Also, even if it is in the public domain, you will still need to inform people if you are using their data for a new process.

Legal claims

Article 9(2)(f) allows for processing in defence of legal claims or 'whenever courts are acting in their judicial capacity'. This is similar to the Schedule 3 section 6 condition for processing.

Substantial public interest

Article 9(2)(g) introduces a new condition for processing that was not available in the DPA, by allowing processing where it is necessary for reasons of substantial public interest. Public health is given as an example of public interest in the recitals[7] even though this gets its own article (see below), but another example explicitly included is processing of political opinions by political parties.[8] However, the usual caveats relating to proportional use, data subject rights and safeguarding the interests of data subjects are included, so if you are using this condition for processing you will have to demonstrate that all these things have been thought through.

Occupational health

Article 9(2)(h) covers processing of health information for occupational health purposes, specifically for managing health data at a society level more generally. Article 9(3) specifically allows for the processing of this information by medical professionals.

Public health

Article 9(2)(i) covers processing in the interests of public health. This allows for processing of personal data across borders to control threats to health, ensuring high quality of health services and medicinal products and devices. The usual safeguarding of individual rights is included, but professional secrecy is also included.

Processing for archival and research purposes

The last condition is in Article 9(2)(j) and is also a new category of processing. This allows for processing for archival purposes or historical, scientific or statistical research purposes. This means that archives and researchers can cite this condition for their work, as long as they keep due regard for the principles of data protection and data subject rights.

Data controllers, joint data controllers and data processors

The DPA already separated data controllers, the organization or body that determines what data will be processed and why from data processors, who will process the data on behalf of the data controller.

The GDPR keeps the distinction between the two types of users of personal data. It adds a situation where two or more controllers are equally determining what happens with personal data. In the GDPR data controllers are defined as

> the natural or legal person, public authority, agency or other body which, alone or jointly with others, determines the purposes and means of the processing of personal data; where the purposes and means of such processing are determined by Union or Member State law, the controller or the specific criteria for its nomination may be provided for by Union or Member State law.[9]

Data processors are defined as 'a natural or legal person, public authority, agency or other body which processes personal data on behalf of the controller'.[10] So the main distinction between a data controller and a data processor is that the data controller determines what should happen with personal data, while the data processor simply carries out the data controller's orders relating to it. So another organization will be a joint data controller if it has just as much say about how and why data is processed, and it will be a data processor if it does not.

The main difference between the GDPR and the DPA when it comes to data processors is the level of responsibility that processors have. Under the DPA, data controllers always bore responsibility for breaches, even if the fault for the breach was with the data processor. This is not the case under the GDPR. Article 82(1) lays out the ability to claim compensation for material and non-material damage from both data controllers and data processors. Article 83 makes it clear that processors can be liable for fines, as well as controllers.

Article 82(2) gives the conditions under which compensation can be claimed, which are different for data controllers and data processors: 'Any controller involved in processing shall be liable for the damage caused by processing which infringes this Regulation. A processor shall be liable for the damage caused by processing only where it has not complied with obligations of this Regulation specifically directed to processors or where it has acted outside or contrary to lawful instructions of the controller.'[11]

Due to 'contrary to lawful instructions of the controller', it is important for data controllers to be clear in their instructions to data processors about how personal data is managed. It is better to use a contract, no matter how brief, that sets out what the personal data is to be used for, where it should be stored, who is allowed access and how it should be destroyed when the processor is no longer required to process the data. Having such a contract will help, should a data processor breach the Regulation without the controller's knowledge.

> NHS Surrey was fined £200,000 when over 3000 patient records were found on a second-hand computer, which should have been destroyed by a data destruction company by industrial guillotine. Written assurance that the hard drives would be destroyed was received, but there was no contract. It is possible that, as NHS Surrey was the data controller, under the DPA it would have been responsible anyway, but a contract might have lessened the fine.

Under the GDPR, which offers an obvious way for data controllers to make data processors responsible, to not have a contract for personal data processing would not be sensible. As a data processor, it would also be in your interests to have a contract in case the data controller was at fault so that you could point to their instructions if a breach should occur.

Data controller responsibilities

Data controllers need to:

- implement data privacy by design and by default;[12]
- determine arrangements with joint data controllers and data processors (as set out above);
- record data processing activities;
- notify the ICO and data subjects of data breaches (see the section on data breaches above);
- co-operate with the ICO or other supervisory authorities;
- keep processing secure (Article 32 is discussed above with principle 6);
- conduct Data Protection Impact assessments (see Chapter 6);
- appoint a DPO in certain circumstances;
- keep to approved codes of conduct;
- show compliance via certification and seals.

Data processors also hold most of these responsibilities.

Registration?

This does not include the registration required by the DPA. The GDPR removed the need to register with the ICO, which removed the fee that registration required. This left the ICO with a funding gap that the UK government did not want to plug.

The result is a set of regulations that are being introduced by the Digital Economy Act 2017. These are the Data Protection (Charges and Information) Regulations 2018. This sets out three tiers of fee as follows:

(a) tier 1 (micro organizations), is £40;
(b) tier 2 (small and medium organizations), is £60;
(c) tier 3 (large organizations), is £2,900.[13]

Tier 1 organizations cover those with a turnover less than or equal to £632,000, or ten or fewer employees, or a charity or small occupational pension. Tier 2 includes organizations with a turnover less than or equal to £36 million or with 11–250 or less employees. Tier 3 organizations are outside both of those categories.

So, organizations will still have to pay a fee, but will not have to register. The information about what personal data you hold should be in an information asset register (IAR) or in another record.

Privacy by design and default

Article 25 sets out the requirements to ensure that the processing of personal data is done with the least amount of data required and keeping the data protection principles and data subject rights in mind. Data should be made available only on a need-to-know basis.

Recording data processing

Article 30 sets out the record-keeping requirements relating to personal data, which are more stringent than the previous registration requirements. Many organizations have either adapted their IARs or started developing them to record what personal data is being held, where, by whom, under what lawful basis and for how long. If you do not want a formal IAR, the ICO has developed a template on how to keep these records.[14]

Co-operating with the ICO and other supervisory authorities

Article 31 covers this requirement, which is pretty much as it is now. Your main responsibility will be to respond to the ICO if they request any information from you relating to a complaint.

Data Protection Officer

Articles 37, 38 and 39 cover when a DPO is needed, what position they should take and what their duties are.

If your organization is a public authority or public body and/or processes large amounts of personal data and/or processes a large amount of special categories or criminal-related personal data, then your organization needs to appoint a DPO. For smaller organizations this does not need to be a single staff member focused on data protection, but can be one individual shared between several organizations. Public authorities are expected to have one staff member in this post.

The DPO is in many ways an internal audit type of role. Controllers and processors are required to allow the DPO to know about data processing activities and to have access to the knowledge and training required to perform the role. The role is protected – you cannot be fired for carrying out your tasks – and you should be able to report directly to senior management. The DPO should be the point of contact for data subjects.

DPO tasks include advising on data protection, carrying out data protection impact assessments, raising awareness and training of staff and being the point of contact for the ICO.

Should you become the DPO? In the end this is a personal decision, but the requirement that DPOs were individually fined for breaches of the GDPR was dropped from the text. The protected nature of the role and the ability to report directly to senior management will (hopefully) give DPOs the authority they need to ensure that the organization can be moved in the direction of better data protection compliance. If you are working in this area and have the possibility of becoming DPO, I think it will be best to take it on.

Codes of conduct and certification

Articles 40 and 41 cover codes of conduct relating to GDPR and Articles 42 and 43 cover certification, including seals.

Codes of conduct are intended to help organizations to apply the GDPR. Certification, including seals, is intended to help show compliance with the GDPR. There are no codes of conduct or certification that are GDPR compliant as of September 2018, but these are likely to be published on the ICO website when they are.

As such, these are things that you will have to look out for as GDPR is implemented and matures.

Conclusion

Now that you have finished this chapter, you should know:

- what the difference is between an EU regulation and a Directive;
- what personal data is;
- what a data subject is;
- what the DP principles are and how to apply them;
- what the lawful bases are for processing;
- how to recognise special categories data and their lawful bases;
- the differences between data controllers and data processors.

For the rights of data subjects, including the sorts of requests you are likely to receive from them, see Chapter 5.

For the types of enquiries you are likely to receive from colleagues, and the internal processes you will have to consider for processing and transferring personal data, see Chapter 6.

5

Data protection: rights of data subjects

This chapter includes the types of requests that data subjects can make relating to data held and processed by a data controller and data processor. The basics of data protection are covered in Chapter 4 and the types of enquiries likely to be raised by staff, including data protection impact assessments and transfers outside the EU, are covered in Chapter 6.

Introduction

This chapter covers the types of requests that you are likely to deal with as a Data Protection Officer (DPO) or in helping the DPO at your organization.

Individuals have been able to request data about themselves under the Data Protection Act (DPA). This right is strengthened in the General Data Protection Regulations (GDPR), although there is now also the possibility of refusing a request if it is manifestly unreasonable, which was not available in the DPA. Under the DPA, you had 40 days to respond.

Data subjects also had the right to get their incorrect information corrected or deleted under the DPA if the data controller did not have a reason to keep it. Data subjects could also object to marketing or automated processing. You had 21 days to respond to these types of requests under the DPA. These rights have also been strengthened in the GDPR and a right to data portability (see below) has been added.

Under the GDPR, all requests from data subjects must be responded to within one month. At the time of writing, there is no guidance as to what this length of time is in days. In UK law, there is a definition of a month, as given in *Halsbury's Laws of England*:[1]

> When the period prescribed is a calendar month running from any arbitrary date the period expires with the day in the succeeding month immediately preceding the day corresponding to the date upon which the period starts: save that, if the period starts at the end of a calendar month which contains more days than the next succeeding month, the period expires at the end of the latter month.

So it could mean you have 28 days to respond in February, 31 days in March and 30 days in April, unless you receive the request on 31 March, which gives you only until 30 April to respond. It would have been easier if a day limit had been adopted, e.g. 28 or 30 days. The ICO has issued advice that a month will mean from the day after the request is received to the same date in the next month, for example 2 June to 2 July for a request received on 1 June. If a request is received on the last day of a month, it is the last day of the next month that becomes the response date.

Recording requests

Unlike FoI and EIR requests, which are similar enough to record on the one system, you will have to record data protection requests separately. The variables relating to data protection requests are not as straightforward as for the other two pieces of legislation.

Subject access requests far outweighed the other types of requests under the DPA, but with the publicity surrounding the right to be forgotten (deletion), particularly, this could change. So you may need to change the way you record requests under the GDPR so that you can include:

- the name and other identifying details of the data subject:
  - for example, you might use an ID number for staff, customers, etc.;
- what sort of request they are making:
  - subject access, deletion, portability, rectification, objection to

  marketing, objection to automated processing or a combination thereof, so do not make this a one-choice-only field;
  - subject access itself has several components, so it is worth recording if the data subject has requested copies of only this data or any of the other elements listed in Article 15(1) (see below);
- other information that helps to identify the information requested:
  - not all requests are for everything a data controller holds, some data subjects are looking for something specific;
- date received;
- date for response;
- date responded;
- a notes field: as large as you can make it, because you are likely to make a lot of notes – at least with certain requests.

How to record what the response actually was is set out below in the section on providing the response.

Subject access requests: what you have to provide

The GDPR sets out the right of access in Article 15. Article 15(3) specifies that 'The controller shall provide a copy of the personal data undergoing processing. For any further copies requested by the data subject, the controller may charge a reasonable fee based on administrative costs. Where the data subject makes the request by electronic means, and unless otherwise requested by the data subject, the information shall be provided in a commonly used electronic form.'[2] Article 15(1) lists other elements that the data subject has a right to know about which includes:

> (a) the purposes of the processing;
> (b) the categories of personal data concerned;
> (c) the recipients or categories of recipient to whom the personal data have been or will be disclosed, in particular recipients in third countries or international organizations;
> (d) where possible, the envisaged period for which the personal data will be stored, or, if not possible, the criteria used to determine that period;
> (e) the existence of the right to request from the controller rectification

or erasure of personal data or restriction of processing of personal data concerning the data subject or to object to such processing;

(f) the right to lodge a complaint with a supervisory authority;

(g) where the personal data are not collected from the data subject, any available information as to their source;

(h) the existence of automated decision-making, including profiling, referred to in Article 22(1) and (4) and, at least in those cases, meaningful information about the logic involved, as well as the significance and the envisaged consequences of such processing for the data subject.[3]

You will need to make it clear to data subjects that they can request this information. However, some of this may already be accessible via an IAR or otherwise already provided to the data subject, e.g. through a privacy notice. While there will always be data subjects who want to know absolutely everything about what you are doing with their data, it is most likely that the vast majority of requesters will be concerned with receiving copies of their data only. Providing all of the other information proactively may not be necessary and would actually be a hindrance to some data subjects who just want a copy of what you are holding.

Subject access requests: scoping the request for copies of personal data

Subject access is the way for people to request their own information. This is where the definition of personal data becomes important. Personal data is defined as

> any information relating to an identified or identifiable natural person ('data subject'); an identifiable natural person is one who can be identified, directly or indirectly, in particular by reference to an identifier such as a name, an identification number, location data, an online identifier or to one or more factors specific to the physical, physiological, genetic, mental, economic, cultural or social identity of that natural person.[4]

A subject access request will potentially cover all such information.

However, a data subject may not necessarily want all of this information, at least at one particular time. They may ask for your organization to focus on one particular area, or certain individuals who might hold the information wanted. For example, an individual who wants copies of a reference may not want any other information you hold on them. To provide everything, particularly within the space of one month, may be as much a waste of their time as yours.

As such, you can offer a form which helps people to narrow down what they want from your organization. They may still end up asking for everything, in which case you have to provide it, but if you are aware that data subjects tend to be asking for one thing only, you can offer them the chance to limit their search to that. It is also via a form that you can make data subjects aware of the other Article 15(1) information they can request and give them a chance to say if they want it or not.

As with the DPA, you can request identification if you are uncertain that it is the data subject themselves who is making the request.[5]

You may have heard of the Durant[6] case, which limited personal data to biographical data or information where the data subject was the focus. 'Mere mention of a name'[7] in a document was not considered to be personal data for the purpose of providing a response to a subject access request. This no longer applies, due to the new definition, which specifically mentions name as a type of personal data. So, a document which includes a name will be considered within scope for a subject access request.

This means that an e-mail newsletter that includes the data subject's name or e-mail address is as much personal data as a personnel file or a medical report. If the request is for everything held, such an e-mail would have to be included. This might mean providing more information than a data subject actually wants, but by including such items you will be showing the breadth and depth of information held, which will help with any complaints to the Information Commissioner.

If you receive multiple requests from the same individual, you do not have to provide copies of information you have already provided without also requiring that a fee is paid. This is covered by Article 15(3), which allows for a reasonable fee for providing copies of information already provided. What is a reasonable fee is not specifically defined, but has to relate to administrative costs. However, it is likely to be composed of the staff time taken to provide the information and any disbursements like photocopying, postage, etc. If you are providing further copies of electronic information, the fee may not necessarily be very high as it may just mean forwarding the information to the individual once again, which is unlikely to take much time or effort. Otherwise a fee cannot be charged for requests made for a subject access request.[8]

Manifestly unreasonable requests

However, Article 12(5) covers what happens when a request is 'manifestly unfounded or excessive, in particular because of their repetitive character'. A data controller can either:

(a) charge a reasonable fee taking into account the administrative costs of providing the information or communication or taking the action requested; or
(b) refuse to act on the request.[9]

This is the first time that data controllers have had the power to refuse a subject access request. It will be worth looking at the guidance on vexatiousness for FoI or manifestly unreasonable requests for the EIR as to the thresholds for refusing a subject access request, but the clue provided in the GDPR is that it is particularly intended for repeated requests where you have already provided everything you hold but the data subject insists that there must be something more. You are required by Article 12(4) to 'inform the data subject without delay and at the latest within one month of receipt of the request of the reasons for not taking action and on the possibility of lodging a complaint with a supervisory authority and seeking a judicial remedy'.

Subject access requests: providing the response

The main difficulty in providing a response for a subject access request is in ensuring that you have provided all the information requested, and that you can track what you provided. Unlike FoI and EIR responses which tend to include the information requested as part of the request, providing copies of information from disparate sources can be harder to track, which becomes an issue when trying to clarify what was provided prior to litigation. Another difficulty can arise when multiple requests are received over a period of time.

Searching for personal data

You will have a month to respond under the GDPR, which is a shorter time period than the 40 days allowed under the DPA. So, having scoped what you have to provide, you have a combination of choices to find the information:

1. Database searches: if there are specific databases that your organization uses which you know are likely to hold data about the data subject, a search of these should be undertaken. Some basic reports from databases can be hard to interpret for people who do not know the systems well, so it will be worth working with the database specialists to produce a report from the database that provides all the information it holds on an individual, but that can still be read by that individual. If you know that a data subject would not be on a database (for example, you would not have customer details on a staff database), then you could exclude those databases from your search even if the request is for everything held.
2. Paper filing systems: if you hold a paper file on an individual that is recognisably about that individual, it would be included within the scope and a copy should be provided. This could be a photocopy or a scan of the file. The latter of these would be more appropriate if all the other information requested is in electronic form. Information held within unstructured paper files, that is, files that are not focused on the individual, are still outside the scope of the GDPR as they were for the DPA, so you do not have to look through all paper files. However, hiding information in unstructured paper files to circumvent providing the information is not allowed.[10]
3. E-mail systems: this is where processing a subject access request can become difficult, and this is not necessarily just in conducting a search. E-mails can also contain third-party information which needs to be redacted before providing the information (how to do this is discussed below).
   a. Searches can be difficult if the data subject has a common first name and surname. You also need to allow for initials or (worse) nicknames or other identifiers relating to the data subject, which can mean that it can be hard to pull together all

of the e-mails relating to the data subject.

b Under the DPA e-mails had to be provided only if they met the Durant definition of personal data, which made sorting through them more difficult. Now that we have to provide everything where a data subject's name is mentioned, this may actually get easier.

c You will receive a lot of e-mail chains from different people with the same e-mails nested in them. You can either provide the data subject with each e-mail including each chain, or try to identify the biggest chain and provide that one only.

d You are likely to receive a mix of printed-out and electronic e-mails. The printed-out e-mails can be easier to redact, but it may be harder to keep track of what you sent out.

e You will also need to watch out for e-mails that refer to an attachment, but where the only copy you have of that e-mail no longer has the attachment. Trying to trace the attachments requires careful searching.

f Some people will send you e-mails with the e-mails about that data subject as individual attachments. Others will send you zip files or other collections. If you save them to a shared filing system, they are likely to lose their date metadata. And if you cannot save them all at the same time, due to the size of the e-mail files, the shared filing system could decide that you are trying to write over the previous files and refuse to let you save any further items. Saving e-mails one by one is very tedious, but it may be your only option.

4 Electronic filing systems – e.g. electronic document and records management system (EDRMS) or SharePoint sites – will have similar issues to e-mail systems for searches for common names, but the documents themselves should be more discrete. You will still, however, have to check for third-party information and redact it.

5 Shared filing systems will be similar to EDRMS, although the search may not be as accurate.

Depending on the electronic filing system you use, you may be able to do a global search over e-mail and shared files. This should not be carried out without a paper trail – for example, a form signed off by a senior manager – or without staff knowing that you may need to conduct such searches from time to time. Global searches will be easier to conduct on unusual names rather than common names, as the latter searches will produce too much noise to signal. Global searches can be useful, however, when you have already provided a lot of information to the data subject and want to show that you have been thorough in your searching.

In most of the searches above you will be relying on the individual staff member to conduct a search of their own e-mail and document stores. The staff member in charge of the database is likely to provide that report, although you may be given access as the DPO to conduct your own searches.

It is worth getting people to provide as many identifiers as you need to conduct the search. The more unique they are, e.g. customer number, the more likely it is that you will have the right person's information. Be careful to check that you have the right person where they have a common or duplicated name.

Redaction/extraction

Having received the results of searches, you will have to look through the material to check that there is no third-party information in it. This is implied by Article 15(4): 'The right to obtain a copy referred to in paragraph 3 shall not adversely affect the rights and freedoms of others.' In other words, you cannot provide a third party's data to another data subject without being certain that you can include it – and in most cases you will not be able to include it. So, you will need to redact the information, i.e. remove it by blacking out.

Paper documents are, in a way, easier to redact. For large sections of text, you can use paper, cardboard or other such material to block out the bits of the document that you cannot include and then photocopy the document. On copies of documents you can use black marker pen to delete words and sentences that cannot be included before photocopying them. Check the photocopy, as sometimes the black marker pen still allows for words to be recognisable. You may have to use black marker pen on the photocopy and then do a second photocopy to be on the safe side. It is useful to keep a copy of the original and the redacted versions so that you can tell what was removed.

Electronic documents are harder to redact, although there are tools available. Documents produced by word processing applications are fairly easy to redact, as you can delete text and/or replace it quite easily. For example, you can include '[Redacted – third-party nformation]' where the third-party text was. E-mails can be harder to redact. You can forward the e-mail to yourself, having redacted the text, although this does make the e-mail one that you have sent to yourself rather than the original that shows who sent and who received it. Another form of redaction can be found in a software package like Adobe Acrobat, which allows you to mark text for redaction and saves a new copy of the redacted PDF document. You can also bundle e-mails for a request together in Adobe Acrobat and can redact each one separately, though it is a slightly fiddly process.

For some documents it is easier to extract the relevant data rather than redact or delete the data you do not need to supply. If a data subject is included in a long list of names in a spreadsheet or other document, it can be better simply to copy their line than delete all the others.

Providing the response

Like for FoI, it is useful to have a basic template or form of words that will serve as a cover letter for the response. If you use a form, it is worth listing the categories on the form to show what you have included.

For e-mailed responses involving large numbers of e-mails and documents, you may run into the size problem. This is where the size of attachments you want to provide could cause you problems, as compared to the number. A large number of small attachments that will still fit through whatever pipe your organization allows for e-mail attachments will be fine. But if you have a 10GB limit on the size of the attachments you can send, being one byte over could stop you from sending the attachments. You can use zip files, but even these can exceed the size you are able to send. So you may have to send multiple e-mails with smaller numbers of attachments to get the material to the data subject.

Another alternative is to use an online transfer service. These allow you to put a large file in a secure place and then tell the data subject how to access it. Only they should be able to access the data, which will then be deleted from its temporary storage space once they have downloaded it. If your organization does not provide such a service, it is worth asking if they will. The organization I work for provides FileDrop, which works very well, although you may have to use a different browser to your normal one in order to use it.

Article 12 makes clear that electronic requests should receive an electronic response.[11] Data subjects can request oral transmission of the data, but you should provide it in that way only if you are certain of the data subject's identity.[12]

Extension to response time

You can take longer than one month, up to two further months, for very large and complex requests. You need to inform the data subject of the reason for the delay.[13] This will be helpful in dealing with those requests that are for everything.

Managing multiple requests

For certain data subjects, you may receive more than one request, particularly where there is an ongoing dispute. It is worth keeping a list on a spreadsheet of:

- what was requested;
- which staff members were mentioned and when their responses were received by you;
- when you sent the response to the data subject for that part of the request.

Having the list helps if there is a complaint to the ICO, as it shows what responses you have been providing. It should also help with providing proof regarding manifestly unreasonable requests (see below).

While one overall case folder is usual per data subject, you can end up with more than one for this type of data subject. Recording the different case numbers on the sheet will help to keep track of the folders you set up. It will also help to gather the final responses together in order to provide them to lawyers, should the data subject also be in dispute with your organization. Lawyers will usually want to see what a data subject has seen.

Restrictions for subject access

Schedules 2, 3 and 4 in the DPA 2018 set out the exact exemptions (restrictions) to subject access allowed in the UK.

This follows Article 23 which allowed member states to exempt data for release under the following categories:

(a) national security;
(b) defence; [the DPA exemption included the armed forces specifically]
(c) public security;
(d) the prevention, investigation, detection or prosecution of criminal offences or the execution of criminal penalties, including the safeguarding against and the prevention of threats to public security;
(e) other important objectives of general public interest of the Union or of a Member State, in particular an important economic or financial interest of the Union or of a Member State, including monetary, budgetary and taxation matters, public health and social security;
(f) the protection of judicial independence and judicial proceedings;
(g) the prevention, investigation, detection and prosecution of breaches of ethics for regulated professions;
(h) a monitoring, inspection or regulatory function connected, even occasionally, to the exercise of official authority in the cases referred to in points (a), (b), (c), (d), (e) and (g);
(i) the protection of the data subject or the rights and freedoms of others;
(j) the enforcement of civil law claims.[14]

Article 23(j) looks to cover legal professional privilege for litigation purposes. However, other exemptions in the DPA 1998 which were absent from the GDPR, have been included in the DPA 2018, such as:

- management information;
- personal data relating to negotiations;
- personal data relating to references, where the receiving data

controller has to release, but the originating data controller can exempt from release;

- 'Personal data relating to an individual's physical or mental health, in certain circumstances and only if granting subject access would be likely to cause serious harm to the physical or mental health of the individual or someone else;
- Personal data that consists of educational records or relates to social work;
- Personal data relating to human fertilisation and embryology, adoption records and reports, statements of a child's special educational needs and parental order records and reports;
- Personal data processed for, or in connection with, a corporate finance service involving price-sensitive information;
- Examination marks and personal data contained in examination scripts;
- Personal data processed for the purposes of making judicial, crown, or ministerial appointments or for conferring honours'.[15]

The Data Protection Act 2018, which replaces the 1998 Act, is drafted to include these further exemptions and has added some allowed for in the derogations, regarding immigration.

One restriction that definitely did not exist in the DPA 1998 was the right to refuse manifestly unreasonable requests, which is discussed above.

All of the exemptions in Article 23 and the time limit of one month also apply to the other data subject rights, which are discussed below.

Requests for rectification

Article 16 gives a right for personal data to be corrected or to be appended to: 'The data subject shall have the right to obtain from the controller without undue delay the rectification of inaccurate personal data concerning him or her. Taking into account the purposes of the processing, the data subject shall have the right to have incomplete personal data completed, including by means of providing a supplementary statement.'

This is no different to before the GDPR. Data subjects have had the right to do this under the DPA. In practical terms, this means correcting data that is incorrect, e.g. changing a spelling of a name to the right spelling or, where you have reason to keep the original data, to add further information to it to reflect the data subject's opinion of the original data. The latter can happen in the case of interview notes or investigation reports where you may have been told something by a witness that the data subject objects to. This does not mean that you have to change the witness statement to the data subject's version of events. However, you can offer to append their version of events to the original witness statement so that they can both be read together.

You are required to let data subjects know when you have rectified their information, unless this would be a disproportionate effort. What disproportionate effort would involve is not yet certain, but it is likely to be large numbers of data subjects and/or a dataset that you got from a third party where you have no contact details for the individuals concerned. This requirement to notify unless disproportionate effort is involved also covers the rights to deletion and restriction.

Requests for deletion: the right to be forgotten

Like rectification, there has always been a right to ask for personal data to be deleted that is no longer required by the data controller, particularly in the case of contact details (see the section on objections to marketing below).

The GDPR right is also more limited than it might appear. Personal data should be deleted on request, if it fits the following categories:

(a) the personal data are no longer necessary in relation to the purposes for which they were collected or otherwise processed;
(b) the data subject withdraws consent on which the processing is based according to point (a) of Article 6(1), or point (a) of Article 9(2), and where there is no other legal ground for the processing;
(c) the data subject objects to the processing pursuant to Article 21(1) and there are no overriding legitimate grounds for the processing, or the data subject objects to the processing pursuant to Article 21(2);
(d) the personal data have been unlawfully processed;
(e) the personal data have to be erased for compliance with a legal obligation in Union or Member State law to which the controller is subject;

(f) the personal data have been collected in relation to the offer of information society services referred to in Article 8(1).[16]

So, the personal data should either no longer be necessary; be provided under the consent condition for processing only; be processed for profiling (Article 21(1)) or marketing (Article 21(2)) purposes; be unlawfully processed; be legally required to be destroyed; or relate to when the data subject was a child on social media in order for the right to be forgotten to be applicable.

As such, it will be worth noting in your IAR the sorts of data where the Article 17 rights would apply. It is one of the reasons why ensuring that you have the right lawful basis for processing is important. If you say that you are keeping personal data due to consent, but you are legally required to keep it, your organization could be in trouble if you get a request for deletion. So, make it clear in privacy notices that you are requesting that the data subject understand that you are processing their data for contractual or legal reasons and that is what they are signing for. In those situations, they are not giving consent.

Can I record that I have deleted data?

Whether you can keep a record of someone's request to be deleted will depend on the circumstances. Some organizations get personal data from third parties, which they then use to update the records they hold. Or systems are fed by other central systems which update details from the central system. If you are in this position and add a record for someone who was previously deleted, this could be considered a breach of the data protection principles. Keeping a 'do not contact' stub would stop such an update because they would already have a record, or a data match would show that person had requested no contact.

However, if the data subject is unlikely ever to appear again in data you hold, deleting all data relating to that data subject would be the best way to ensure that you had met their rights under this article.

Right to restrict processing

Again, like the right to rectification and deletion, there was always a right to restrict processing in the DPA. Restriction is different to deletion or objection to processing and involves:

> Where processing has been restricted under paragraph 1, such personal data shall, with the exception of storage, only be processed with the data subject's consent or for the establishment, exercise or defence of legal claims or for the protection of the rights of another natural or legal person or for reasons of important public interest of the Union or of a Member State.[17]

So, once a legitimate request for restriction is received, you can store it and use it only for legal claims or protection of rights, unless you have the data subject's consent.

Like the right to deletion, this is not an absolute right, but can be requested only in the following circumstances set out in Article 18 (1):

> (a) the accuracy of the personal data is contested by the data subject, for a period enabling the controller to verify the accuracy of the personal data;
> (b) the processing is unlawful and the data subject opposes the erasure of the personal data and requests the restriction of their use instead;
> (c) the controller no longer needs the personal data for the purposes of the processing, but they are required by the data subject for the establishment, exercise or defence of legal claims;
> (d) the data subject has objected to processing pursuant to Article 21(1) pending the verification whether the legitimate grounds of the controller override those of the data subject.[18]

Article 18(1)(a) makes sense if you have had a request for clarification of data required to be processed for a purpose but the data subject does not think this is correct. For example, if the data subject claims that you are sending a regular order to the wrong address, it will save you the time and trouble of dealing with returns or thefts if you verify what the address is.

Article 18(1)(b) allows for a data subject to tell you to stop processing personal data that you do not legally have a right to rather than deleting it. This could possibly be due to litigation – they may want to prove that you had the data that you should not have.

Article 18(1)(c) means that you cannot delete compromising personal data. It is likely that this right could be claimed at the same time that a subject access request is made.

Article 18(1)(d) is where your record keeping relating to the legitimate interests condition for processing is going to be important. It would be worth identifying what your legitimate interests are and keeping this on your IAR. It means that, should you get a request to stop processing you will be able to be clear about why you need to continue processing. Otherwise, the data subject could more easily claim that their rights regarding the data outweigh your legitimate interests in processing it.

Objections to processing

Objections to processing unlike restriction stop all processing of the personal data for a particular purpose. This is set out in Article 21:

1. The data subject shall have the right to object, on grounds relating to his or her particular situation, at any time to processing of personal data concerning him or her which is based on point (e) or (f) of Article 6(1), including profiling based on those provisions. The controller shall no longer process the personal data unless the controller demonstrates compelling legitimate grounds for the processing which override the interests, rights and freedoms of the data subject or for the establishment, exercise or defence of legal claims.
2. Where personal data are processed for direct marketing purposes, the data subject shall have the right to object at any time to processing of personal data concerning him or her for such marketing, which includes profiling to the extent that it is related to such direct marketing.
3. Where the data subject objects to processing for direct marketing purposes, the personal data shall no longer be processed for such purposes.
4. At the latest at the time of the first communication with the data subject, the right referred to in paragraphs 1 and 2 shall be explicitly brought to the attention of the data subject and shall be presented clearly and separately from any other information.
5. In the context of the use of information society services, and

notwithstanding Directive 2002/58/EC, the data subject may exercise his or her right to object by automated means using technical specifications.

6. Where personal data are processed for scientific or historical research purposes or statistical purposes pursuant to Article 89(1), the data subject, on grounds relating to his or her particular situation, shall have the right to object to processing of personal data concerning him or her, unless the processing is necessary for the performance of a task carried out for reasons of public interest.[19]

So, Article 21(1) allows for objections generally relating to the conditions for processing relating to public task (Article 6(1)(e)) or legitimate interests (Article 6(1)(f)) as well as specific objections to marketing in Articles 21(2) and (3). Like the right to restrict processing, your record keeping relating to what the task in the public interest or exercise of official authority is, and/or what your legitimate interests are for processing the data will be important for ensuring that you can quickly and easily show why these reasons outweigh the data subject's rights. You also have a right to keep processing for your own legal claims.

Article 21(4) means that you must tell people about this right the first time you communicate with them.

Article 21(5) appears to mean that if you provide an online service, a data subject should be able to use that service to object to processing.

Article 21(6) allows for data subjects to object to and stop processing of their data for research, unless a researcher can show that this is a task carried out in the public interest. This exemption is similar to Article 6(1)(e), so if the research relates to that sort of processing, it would mean that the research could continue in spite of the objection.

Always cross-reference the Privacy and Electronic Communications Regulations and/or E-privacy Regulations when it comes to marketing, so as to ensure compliance across both regimes (see Chapter 8).

Requests for data portability

Data portability is one of the few areas to get early guidance from the Article 29 Working Party. The Article 29 Working Party is a group set up to advise on data protection at EU level. This is the first completely new right for data subjects and has been set up to help consumers transfer between service providers, for example, if you are moving between telecommunications providers or utilities or other data controllers with similar datasets. The idea is that a data subject can request their data in a machine readable format and take it to a new service provider who can plug it into their systems.

There are three main issues with this right. The first is producing a machine readable version of the data. While some systems will be fairly easy to gather the data from, others will not. The second is to whom do you provide the data? Do you send it to the data subject to then pass on or to the other data controller directly? Do you provide an automated tool to allow data subjects to extract the data themselves? The latter option may cause less contamination to the data, but does open up access to your systems. The last issue is ingesting the data by the new data controller. How do they determine that the data is clean and therefore safe to introduce into their systems? You will need to act closely with your IT department to make certain that systems are capable of supporting the right to data portability.

This is a conditional right which is focused on personal data provided by the data subject. While this is likely to include contact details provided by the data subject, the Article 29 Working Party thinks that this includes use data generated by the data subject, for example raw data created by smart meter usage. However, any analysis that a data controller does of the raw data is not considered to be provided by the data subject, so it is out of scope. You also have to ensure that any data that you provide does not infringe on the rights of others, which the Article 29 Working Party says is likely to include intellectual property and trade secrets.[20]

Like other requests, you have to respond in one month, even if it is to say that you will not be complying with the request, and providing the reasons why you cannot.

Automated processing and profiling

Aside from the extension to profiling, this right also existed under the DPA. You can object to automated processing and ask that a human being reviews the processing where there are 'legal effects concerning him or her or similarly significantly affects him or her'.[21] There are exceptions to this set out in Article 22(2), which include: processing for a contract; legal authorisation to perform the automated processing; and explicit consent of the data subject.

Profiling is defined in Article 4(4) as 'any form of automated processing of personal data consisting of the use of personal data to evaluate certain personal aspects relating to a natural person, in particular to analyse or predict aspects concerning that natural person's performance at work, economic situation, health, personal preferences, interests, reliability, behaviour, location or movements'.[22] It is possible that your organization does not do any profiling, but if there is any such processing and it does not fit into any of the exceptions above, you will have to let data subjects know that you are carrying out such processing and give them the chance to object to it.[23] You should also have a procedure in place to deal with such a request so that you know which staff member(s) will be doing the human review.

You cannot use automated processing or profiling for the special categories of personal data, unless one of the exceptions in Article 9(2)(a) through to (g) applies. These are all the exceptions other than health, public health and research.

Conclusion

Now that you have finished this chapter, you should know:

- how to determine the date of response for a request;
- how to record a request;
- how to process a subject access request;
- how to manage requests for rectification/corrections;
- how to manage requests for deletion;
- how to manage requests to restrict processing and objections to processing;
- what to consider for requests for data portability;
- how to ensure that data subject rights related to automated processing and profiling are managed correctly.

For the basics of data protection, including the difference between a Directive and a Regulation, the data protection principles, special categories of data and the difference between data controllers and data processors, see Chapter 4.

For guidance on managing staff enquiries on data protection, including privacy notices and transfers outside the EEA, see Chapter 6.

6

Data protection: internal enquiries

Introduction

This chapter covers the sorts of enquiries that you are likely to receive from your colleagues about what they need to do when collecting, processing, sharing and otherwise using personal data. I have assumed that readers will be acting as Data Protection Officer (DPO) for their organization, but even if you are not officially in that position or your organization is not required to appoint a DPO, this chapter focuses on advising others within your organization on what their data protection responsibilities are. These are all likely to be internal, although you may need to get involved with contracts with third parties when sharing data. The following are examples of what you will need to advise your colleagues on:

- creating privacy notices and consent forms for collection of data;
- conducting privacy impact assessments – recognising when this is necessary, how to carry them out;
- sharing data with third parties – when you can make transfers to third parties, under what circumstances and how to do so securely;
- enquiries of the type 'can I do this with personal data?', which come in many varieties.

Privacy notices and consent forms

Privacy notices and consent forms have always been required under the Data Protection Act (DPA) when collecting information from data subjects. They are intended to let data subjects know why the data is required, who will see it and what will be done with it. Previously some organizations relied on the one privacy notice for all collections of data. Others created new notices with each collection carried out. The latter are in a better position under the General Data Protection Regulation (GDPR), which set out what details you need to provide to people for data that you collect directly and for data that you receive from third parties. A one-size-fits-all privacy notice will not be compliant with the GDPR.

Articles 13 and 14: Information to be provided to the data subject

Both these articles cover what information a data subject has to be provided with when their data is being used. However, there are differences between when you are collecting the information yourself and when you are using personal data obtained from a third party.

This information needs to be contained in what is called a privacy notice. If you are using a consent form, this will also in practice be a privacy notice. You need to have a separate notice for each separate collection of data. Unless you are processing personal data for one purpose only, a single privacy notice covering all types of personal data processing will not be adequate. However, if the data subject already knows some or all of the points in Table 6.1 you are not required to provide it to them again.

Table 6.1 *Providing information to data subjects*

Information to be provided to data subjects		When information comes directly from the data subject	When information comes from a third party
At the time of collection or receipt of data	The identity and the contact details of the controller and, where applicable, of the controller's representative	Yes, Article 13(1)(a); every time except for the controller's representative.	Yes, Article 14(1)(a); every time except for the controller's representative.
	The contact details of the Data Protection Officer, where applicable	Yes, Article 13(1)(b); only if applicable.	Yes, Article 14(1)(b); only if applicable

(*Continued*)

Table 6.1 *Continued*

Information to be provided to data subjects		**When information comes directly from the data subject**	**When information comes from a third party**
	The purposes of the processing for which the personal data are intended as well as the legal basis for the processing	Yes, Article 13(1)(c); every time	Yes, Article 14(1)(c); every time
	Where the processing is based on point (f) of Article 6(1), the legitimate interests pursued by the controller or by a third party	Yes, Article 13(1)(d); only if applicable	No
	The categories of personal data concerned	No	Yes, Article 14(1)(d); every time
	The recipients or categories of recipients of the personal data, if any	Yes, Article 13(1)(e); only if applicable	Yes, Article 14(1)(e); only if applicable.
	Where applicable, the fact that the controller intends to transfer personal data to a third country or international organization and the existence or absence of an adequacy decision by the Commission, or in the case of transfers referred to in Article 46 or 47, or the second subparagraph of Article 49(1), reference to the appropriate or suitable safeguards and the means by which to obtain a copy of them or where they have been made available	Yes, Article 13(1)(f); only if applicable	Yes, Article 14(1)(f); only if applicable
In order to ensure fair and transparent processing	The period for which the personal data will be stored, or if that is not possible, the criteria used to determine that period	Yes, Article 13(2)(a); every time	Yes, Article 14(2)(a); every time

(*Continued*)

Table 6.1 *Continued*

Information to be provided to data subjects		**When information comes directly from the data subject**	**When information comes from a third party**
	The existence of the right to request from the controller access to and rectification or erasure of pers-onal data or restriction of pro-cessing concerning the data subject or to object to pro-cessing as well as the right to data portability	Yes, Article 13(2)(b); every time	Yes, Article 14(2)(c); every time
	Where the processing is based on point (a) of Article 6(1) or point (a) of Article 9(2), the existence of the right to withdraw consent at any time, without affecting the lawfulness of processing based on consent before its withdrawal	Yes, Article 13(2)(c); if applicable	Yes, Article 14(2)(d); if applicable
	Where the processing is based on point (f) of Article 6(1), the legitimate interests pursued by the controller or by a third party	No	Yes, Article 14(2)(b); if applicable
	The right to lodge a complaint with a supervisory authority	Yes, Article 13(2)(d); every time	Yes, Article 14(2)(e); every time
	Whether the provision of personal data is a statutory or contractual requirement, or a requirement necessary to enter into a contract, as well as whether the data subject is obliged to provide the personal data and of the possible consequences of failure to provide such data	Yes, Article 13(2)(e); if applicable	No

(Continued)

Table 6.1 *Continued*

Information to be provided to data subjects		When information comes directly from the data subject	When information comes from a third party
	From which source the personal data originate, and if applicable, whether it came from publicly accessible sources	No	Yes, Article 14(2)(f); every time and if applicable for public sources
	The existence of automated decision making, including profiling, referred to in Article 22(1) and (4) and, at least in those cases, meaningful information about the logic involved, as well as the significance and the envisaged consequences of such processing for the data subject	Yes, Article 13(2)(f); if applicable	Yes, Article 13(2)(g); if applicable

While the privacy notices for information collected directly can and should be provided at the time of collection, you have up to one month to inform data subjects of personal data obtained from another source.

It will likely be easier to provide this information to people where you are collecting the data directly. Whether the collection is from a paper form that you will use for data entry or from a secure web form, you can add the necessary details to the form where people can see them. If you are conducting interviews, you would normally give interviewees an information sheet so that they know how their data will be used. The interview information sheet can easily include the information required by Article 13. It will be helpful to staff at your organization to provide templates with as much of this information already included as you can.

It is when you have collected data from a third party for re-use that you may have trouble. It may not be so difficult if the dataset contains current contact details, but if you have a historic dataset it may be difficult to let people know. One way could be through the IAR, or however you are keeping records as required by the Regulation. A list of datasets acquired there, publicly available on a website, could meet the requirements of Article 14. The ICO has produced some basic guidance on how to practically meet the requirements of Article 14, for example, using dashboards to allow people to manage what data you hold relating to them or conducting a data protection impact assessment if you intend to rely on the fact that it would be disproportionate to contact everybody.[i]

Privacy notices also need to be pitched at the right level for the intended data subject(s). Simpler language will be needed if you are collecting data from children. If you can, test your proposed privacy notice with people of the same age, background, etc. to the people you wish to collect data from, so as to check that they can understand what you are telling them.

Data protection or privacy impact assessments

This is one area where the guidance has come fairly quickly. Privacy impact assessments were developed by the ICO and encouraged, but have become law for certain types of data processing under the GDPR under the name of 'data protection impact assessments' (DPIA). These are set out in Article 35(1):

> Where a type of processing in particular using new technologies, and taking into account the nature, scope, context and purposes of the processing, is likely to result in a high risk to the rights and freedoms of natural persons, the controller shall, prior to the processing, carry out an assessment of the impact of the envisaged processing operations on the protection of personal data. A single assessment may address a set of similar processing operations that present similar high risks.

A DPIA is essentially about determining the risks of a new or large amount of personal data processing.

Processing using new technologies, or even technologies new to your organization, is fairly clear. If, for example, your organization is considering using biometric data like fingerprint technology for access, although this technology has existed for a while, it would be worth carrying out a DPIA to ensure that the processing was necessary. Access to high-security areas by a small number of staff, or where you have to ensure that you have identified the right individual taking a nursing examination, might justify fingerprint recognition. Using the technology just to allow general access to a building may not be appropriate if less invasive methods like swipe cards are enough.

Working out high risk can be a bit harder. While Article 35(3) in the GDPR sets out some examples, the Article 29 Working Party guidance expands on the list and defines the following as indicating high risk data protection:

1. when using personal data to evaluate or score individuals;
2. when processing personal data could exclude or discriminate against individuals;
3. systematic monitoring, particularly in public areas that individuals cannot avoid appearing in;
4. any processing relating to special categories of data;
5. large-scale processing, which is defined by 'a. the number of data subjects concerned, either as a specific number or as a proportion of the relevant population; b. the volume of data and/or the range of different data items being processed; c. the duration, or permanence, of the data processing activity; d. the geographical extent of the processing activity';[2]
6. when combining datasets – it has been proven that anonymised datasets can be un-anonymised by matching them with another dataset;
7. when processing personal data of vulnerable data subjects. These can be children or those unable to give informed consent. However, it includes any data subjects where there is an unequal balance between the data controller and the data subject, so processing relating to employees could fall under this category;
8. innovative use of technologies, like the fingerprint example above;
9. data transfers to a country without GDPR equivalent protection;
10. processing which interferes with a data subject's rights, for example, where processing will deny a data subject a service like a loan.

Article 35(4) of the GDPR requires the ICO to produce a list of the types of processing that will require a DPIA, while Article 35(5) allows them to produce a list where DPIAs will not be required. Both lists have to take into account other lists produced by other supervisory authorities across the EU.

However, it is up to data controllers to consider if one is needed. The pressure to conduct one may come from outside. You may be required to conduct a DPIA before a data controller will share data with you or before a third party will provide you with a dataset, even if the processing does not fall into the categories listed above.

The Article 28 Working Party guidance also suggested that if processing will continue after the GDPR, then a DPIA should be carried out if the processing fits into any of the above categories. Article 35(11) requires reviews of a DPIA to ensure that processing stays compliant, particularly for any changes made in processing.

Carrying out a data protection impact assessment

So, how should you carry out a DPIA? And when should you start? Who should be involved?

Article 35(7) says that the DPIA

> shall contain at least:
>
> a) a systematic description of the envisaged processing operations and the purposes of the processing, including, where applicable, the legitimate interest pursued by the controller;
> b) an assessment of the necessity and proportionality of the processing operations in relation to the purposes;
> c) an assessment of the risks to the rights and freedoms of data subjects referred to in paragraph 1; and
> d) the measures envisaged to address the risks, including safeguards, security measures and mechanisms to ensure the protection of personal data and to demonstrate compliance with this Regulation taking into account the rights and legitimate interests of data subjects and other persons concerned.

This means taking into account the relevant codes of conduct/codes of practice released by the ICO and equivalent supervising authorities as required by Article 35(12). It is worth using these as a basis for developing a form that you can fill out when you conduct the DPIA.

The ICO Privacy Impact Assessment (PIA) Code of Practice lists the following actions to undertake:

1 Identify a need for a PIA – see above.
2 Describe the information flows – that is, what information is going to be used, where, for what purpose.
3 Identify the privacy and related risks. What are the risks to the data subjects, e.g. will their rights be threatened? What are the risks to the organization, e.g. are there reputational risks if the processing goes wrong? Pages 24–6 of the ICO's PIA Code of Practice list several types of risks to consider.
4 Identify and evaluate privacy solutions. Starting from the list of risks, what will help to ameliorate the risks? Will the risk disappear with the solution, or will it be managed? What are the costs versus the benefits of each solution?
5 Sign-off and recording outcomes. Having chosen the best solutions for each risk, record this and get them signed off by the most appropriate senior manager.
6 Integrate PIA outcomes into the main project plan.

There is also a pre-1 action, which is to consult with internal and external stakeholders to gain their views on the processing before proceeding, which is also required by Article 35(9). One of these stakeholders must be the DPO where designated (Article 35(2)), who is required to advise on the data protection impacts of projects. If you have not yet got into the project planning stage for IT projects at your organization, this is the stick that you can use to find your way in.

The Article 29 Working Party guidance expands on this basic frame by identifying:

- when a DPIA should happen – before processing starts; Processing the data and then identifying the risks involved with doing so will not be looked on favourably;
- who should be involved – the DPO, project manager/team with someone senior enough to sign off on the actions at least informed. Data processors should be included in any assessments;
- how to consult with data subjects, depending on the amount of consultation you intend to carry out. If your organization decides

to process contrary to the wishes of data subjects (but still legally!), you will need to let them know;
- whether you should publish the DPIA;
- when you will need to contact the ICO or appropriate supervisory authority – if there are large residual risks to processing.

If you are not certain where to start, it is worth asking your networks for DPIA or PIA forms that people are already using. The annexes of the ICO Code of Practice are helpful for developing a form from scratch, but examples from your sector may be better tailored and easier to follow. You may want to adapt them for your organization, but it can be easier to work from an example. It is worth following the relevant code of conduct and the Article 29 Working Party guidance very closely the first time you conduct a DPIA. Once you get more used to the language and, in particular, identifying risks and solutions, which is the core of the DPIA, they will become easier to conduct.

Transfers to other countries and within international organizations

Transfers outside the EEA have transformed from a single principle into a full Chapter in its own right in the GDPR. The Chapter covers transfers of personal data to companies outside the EU and within international organizations.

The main purpose of the Chapter is to ensure that as far as possible the personal data of European citizens is treated as if covered by the GDPR, no matter where in the world it is being processed. It is debatable how enforceable this is. However, the main mechanism is to ensure that data controllers within the EU either transfer to countries identified as having adequate protection, contract with companies in other countries to ensure adequate protection or simply do not transfer personal data to those countries. The USA is not considered an adequate country, but both the now defunct Safe Harbor scheme and the current EU–US Privacy Shield intend to allow US companies to say that they will abide by the EU rules in order to do business with EU citizens, particularly for cloud and internet-based services. If you want to use a cloud product, either it has to offer storage within the EU or you have to contract with the service to provide adequate protection. It is unlikely that a data controller will be able to completely ignore this Chapter.

Conditions for processing regarding transfers

Article 44 provides a general principle that transfers can occur 'to a third country or international organization' only if 'the conditions laid down in this Chapter are complied with by the controller and processor, including for onward transfers of personal data from the third country or an international organization to another third country or to another international organization'.[3] These conditions include:

- when a third country is considered to have adequate data protection (Article 45);
- when appropriate safeguards have been used (Article 46);
- when binding corporate rules have been applied within a multinational organization (Article 47);
- where a specific derogation applies (Article 49).

Article 48 prohibits a third country from requiring transfer of personal data for justice or administrative purposes unless an international agreement allows for such a transfer. Article 50 covers international co-operation activities that would support data protection.

Article 45 allows for transfer of personal data to a third country, territory of a country or an international organization that has been recognised as having adequate data protection without the need for specific authorisation. The judgement of adequacy will be carried out by the European Commission. The DPA would not pass the adequacy requirements – one of the reasons why, if you are dealing with personal data of EU citizens, you would need to behave as if you were covered by the GDPR anyway, even if the new DPA did not incorporate the GDPR into UK law.

Article 46 allows for the use of other safeguards, without the need for specific authorisation by the ICO or any other supervisory authority. These are set out in section 2 as:

a) a legally binding and enforceable instrument between public authorities or bodies;

b) binding corporate rules in accordance with Article 47;
c) standard data protection clauses adopted by the Commission in accordance with the examination procedure referred to in Article 93(2);
d) standard data protection clauses adopted by a supervisory authority and approved by the Commission pursuant to the examination procedure referred to in Article 93(2);
e) an approved code of conduct pursuant to Article 40 together with binding and enforceable commitments of the controller or processor in the third country to apply the appropriate safeguards, including as regards data subjects' rights; or
f) an approved certification mechanism pursuant to Article 42 together with binding and enforceable commitments of the controller or processor in the third country to apply the appropriate safeguards, including as regards data subjects' rights.[4]

There are a lot of other articles referred to here, but what they all have in common is using contractual clauses between public bodies, within a company or between two parties based on, generally, an approved set of clauses created by the European Commission or a supervisory authority.

Article 47 shows the sort of information that the EU would require for binding corporate rules in Article 47(2), having had the relevant supervisory authority sign them off.[5] These are included in full below so as to show the scope of what you need to include.

Article 47(2) states that binding corporate rules must include:

a) the structure and contact details of the group of undertakings, or group of enterprises engaged in a joint economic activity and of each of its members;
b) the data transfers or set of transfers, including the categories of personal data, the type of processing and its purposes, the type of data subjects affected and the identification of the third country or countries in question;
c) their legally binding nature, both internally and externally;
d) the application of the general data protection principles, in particular purpose limitation, data minimisation, limited storage periods, data quality, data protection by design and by default, legal basis for

processing, processing of special categories of personal data, measures to ensure data security, and the requirements in respect of onward transfers to bodies not bound by the binding corporate rules;

e) the rights of data subjects in regard to processing and the means to exercise those rights, including the right not to be subject to decisions based solely on automated processing, including profiling in accordance with Article 22, the right to lodge a complaint with the competent supervisory authority and before the competent courts of the Member States in accordance with Article 79, and to obtain redress and, where appropriate, compensation for a breach of the binding corporate rules;
f) the acceptance by the controller or processor established on the territory of a Member State of liability for any breaches of the binding corporate rules by any member concerned not established in the Union; the controller or the processor shall be exempt from that liability, in whole or in part, only if it proves that that member is not responsible for the event giving rise to the damage;
g) how the information on the binding corporate rules, in particular on the provisions referred to in points (d), (e) and (f) of this paragraph is provided to the data subjects in addition to Articles 13 and 14;
h) the tasks of any data protection officer designated in accordance with Article 37 or any other person or entity in charge of the monitoring compliance with the binding corporate rules within the group of undertakings, or group of enterprises engaged in a joint economic activity, as well as monitoring training and complaint-handling;
i) the complaint procedures;
j) the mechanisms within the group of undertakings, or group of enterprises engaged in a joint economic activity for ensuring the verification of compliance with the binding corporate rules. Such mechanisms shall include data protection audits and methods for ensuring corrective actions to protect the rights of the data subject. Results of such verification should be communicated to the person or entity referred to in point (h) and to the board of the controlling undertaking of a group of undertakings, or of the group of enterprises engaged in a joint economic activity, and should be available upon request to the competent supervisory authority;
k) the mechanisms for reporting and recording changes to the rules and reporting those changes to the supervisory authority;

l) the cooperation mechanism with the supervisory authority to ensure compliance by any member of the group of undertakings, or group of enterprises engaged in a joint economic activity, in particular by making available to the supervisory authority the results of verifications of the measures referred to in point (j);
m) the mechanisms for reporting to the competent supervisory authority any legal requirements to which a member of the group of undertakings, or group of enterprises engaged in a joint economic activity is subject in a third country which are likely to have a substantial adverse effect on the guarantees provided by the binding corporate rules; and
n) the appropriate data protection training to personnel having permanent or regular access to personal data.

In Article 47(3) the European Commission reserves the right to specify the format of binding corporate rules, so once you have drafted rules that include all of the above, you may have to review them in the future, should a specific format be legally required.

Article 49 allows for derogations, or exemptions, to the rules relating to international transfers. These include data subject consent due to a contract, public interest, legal claims, vital interests where the data subject is incapable of consent and transfer of information held on public registers. Transfer outside these categories is allowed if

> the transfer is not repetitive, concerns only a limited number of data subjects, is necessary for the purposes of compelling legitimate interests pursued by the controller which are not overridden by the interests or rights and freedoms of the data subject, and the controller has assessed all the circumstances surrounding the data transfer and has on the basis of that assessment provided suitable safeguards with regard to the protection of personal data.[6]

For these non-repetitive transfers you must also inform both the ICO and the data subjects of the transfer.

Dealing with internal enquiries

Unlike FoI and EIR, data protection is not just about providing information, but about determining how you are processing personal data and being transparent to data subjects about how you are using it. This means that a DPO will be answering lots of different enquiries. This involves trying to balance what the text of the law says, the interpretations of the law provided by the ICO and other supervisory authorities, the rights of the data subject(s) and the needs of the organization.

Some examples of the sorts of enquiries you can deal with are listed below.

- Can we use CCTV in an internal area to identify a thief?
- How do we get parental consent/knowledge for programmes involving schoolchildren when we deal with schools, rather than the parents directly?
- How do we legally track the entry of a prisoner allowed under licence to attend our courses?
- Is this cloud computing contract compliant with data protection?
- Can we sign this data sharing agreement with organization X?
- Am I allowed to provide personal data to the Police, and under what circumstances?
- How far am I allowed to disclose disability data within our organization or outside it?
- We are being sent disability information internally that we don't need to see. Is this a breach of the data subjects' rights?

Some enquiries you will be able to answer from experience. Others will require checking with the guidance and the actual legislation. I'll use two of the examples from above to show how to advise staff what they should do in order to be compliant.

Using CCTV in an internal area to identify a thief

If you search the GDPR, you will not find a reference to CCTV or cameras. Nor to video or photographs. The Data Protection Act 1998 also comes up blank for those terms. The Data Protection Act 2018 mentions only photographs, and that is in relation to indecent photographs of children. Yet these are personal data, and very much identifying personal data as they reproduce a person's appearance either at one point in time or at the time the camera is operating. So, in this case the Regulation and Act do not provide much in the way of specific guidance for when you should or should not use CCTV or how you should be using it.

In this case, you will have to turn to the ICO guidance, which is in the form of a Code of Practice. This also refers to the Surveillance Camera Code of Practice, which is produced by the Surveillance Camera Commissioner as a requirement of the Protection of Freedoms Act,[7] which covers England and Wales only. The Code of Practice takes you through making a decision on whether to introduce CCTV, through to how to store, share (where necessary) and dispose of the images.

The Code of Practice takes you through a series of questions to determine if CCTV is necessary, so you need to ask what you have tried before and determine why this has not worked. Then, having decided that CCTV is truly necessary, you need to determine for how long it needs to run (24 hours? overnight? working hours only?) and who will have access to the images – e.g. security staff only. When you put the cameras up, are they pointing at the right place? Do you let people know that you are using CCTV as a deterrent, or is this a truly covert use where the object is to provide evidence, so that once you have evidence you will stop using the cameras? If you haven't collected evidence by a certain time, are you going to stop using the cameras? When will you destroy the footage?

In this case it could be that you are concerned that someone with normal access to an office area is the thief and access logs have not allowed you to determine whom this might be. The thefts have led to money and other property being taken on multiple occasions. The thefts are happening overnight. Your organization wants to gather video evidence to identify the thief. The cameras are intended to run overnight only, not during normal office hours, and will cover the areas of the office where the thefts have been occurring and not point outside the room. Only security staff will view the footage unless there is a need to disseminate an image more widely in the organization to identify the alleged thief. The cameras will run until the thief is caught in the act or by the end of three months, whichever is sooner. As the purpose is to catch the thief, there will be no notices to show that CCTV is in use.

As DPO, you could advise that this use is proportionate. It is for a specific purpose and time period and has considered the rights of staff not to be surveilled while they work. However, this example shows the level of detail that you need to consider as to whether CCTV should be used or not. You could use a PIA to track your decisions, but if you don't want to go that far it would still be worth recording somewhere how you came to your position.

How do we legally track the entry of a prisoner allowed under licence to attend our courses?

The situation presented to you is that a prisoner has been granted licence to attend a course at your institution; however, the prison wants to ensure attendance, otherwise the licence will be revoked. Is there a lawful basis for providing the data to the prison?

In this case, you will have to look at Article 6 and potentially Article 9 of the GDPR. The first question to ask is what data is being requested to be transferred to the prison. At first glance, because the data subject is a prisoner, you may think of the special categories of data relating to criminal convictions. However, that is not the personal data sought. The data sought relates to what can prove attendance at the course. So this could be using an ID card for entry into the building or extracts from attendance logs. This means that only an Article 6 basis will apply: consent, contract, legal reasons, vital interests, public task, legitimate interests.

Vital interests does not cover the processing (the prisoner will not live or die without it), although you could argue that it is in their non-vital interests to prove that they are attending. Public task and legitimate interests (depending on whether you are a public or private institution) also do not cover the processing: it is likely neither to be a public duty to provide the data nor in the organization's interests to process it unless you could argue that the fee for the course is covered by legitimate interests. It is not really about entering into or processing for a contract, as the contract is with the student, not the prison. Consent cannot be obtained where there is an imbalance in the power arrangement. The prisoner is not able to give consent freely because the data has to be provided, otherwise they break the terms of the licence. There is an element of coercion that does not meet the requirements of consent in the GDPR.

This means that legal reasons is the most likely lawful basis for processing. Under the terms of a licence, legally required by the prison service in order for the prisoner to attend, the organization can provide the attendance data to the prison.

Handling enquiries summary

When you get an enquiry, consider it within the following framework:

- Does the situation actually involve personal data? Can the task be done without processing personal data?
- If it does involve personal data, is this 'normal' personal data or special categories?
- If it is about collection of personal data, what is the lawful basis?
- What are data subjects being told about collection? Are they being told about collection of their data?
- If the information needs to be shared, is this a one-off sharing of data or a regular sharing of data? What data sharing agreement exists, if any? If there is no data sharing agreement, does there need to be?
- Where is data being stored? Are there any security concerns? Bring in your information security colleagues here, if you have to.
- Is the processing of data new or particularly invasive? Should an impact assessment be carried out?

Also, remember to go back to the text of the Regulation and any associated Acts. This will help to ensure that any advice you give is based on the legislation rather than on guidance, which is always less distinct.

Responding to the ICO

Not all data subjects will be happy with the way you deal with their requests. You will also need to report data breaches and deal with any follow-up to that.

With data subject complaints, acknowledge that the complaint has come in and say up front if you will have any issues with responding to the fairly short deadlines that you will be given by the ICO. If a key staff member is not available, say so, and when they will be available. Then respond by the time you said you would.

Some complainants will believe that the information you provided was not enough. In those cases, you will need to provide details of the searches you have undertaken and give some proof of the likelihood of where information will be and why it is most likely that you do not hold anything further. If you have answered multiple requests, a spreadsheet listing each request and what was provided is a useful thing to provide to show how thorough you have been.

Some complainants will be querying your use of exemptions or redactions. You will need to provide proof of why the exemption applies. If you have redacted third-party information, you can provide the ICO with the originals to show that you have removed only data relating to those third parties.

When it comes to breaches, look carefully at each question you are given and answer them, rather than the question you might prefer to. If it is impossible to answer a particular question, say so.

The ICO takes data subjects' rights to information very seriously. So be prepared to make your case. You can involve solicitors if you want them to act on your behalf, which may be necessary if the subject access requests are part of a bigger complaint or grievance and your solicitors have been handling the other aspects of the case.

Conclusion

Now that you have finished this chapter, you should know:

- what to put in a privacy notice to ensure that data subjects know what you are doing with their data;
- how to carry out a data protection impact assessment;
- what you have to consider when transferring data outside the EEA;
- how to log requests, including working out time periods;
- how to work through the many internal requests you will receive from staff.

For the basics of data protection, including the difference between a Directive and a Regulation, the data protection principles, special categories data and the difference between data controllers and data processors, see Chapter 4.

For information on how to respond to data subject requests, including requests for deletion, stopping or objecting to processing, rectification and portability, see Chapter 5.

7

Environmental Information Regulations

Introduction

This chapter covers what environmental information is and how to respond to requests for environmentally related information. This is because environmental information is covered by separate regulations to the Freedom of Information (FoI) Acts. If you are the one processing FoI requests, you need to know about the EIR, as you will be processing these requests as well as a matter of course.

The EIR are a lot like the Freedom of Information Acts (FoIAs), until they are not. The same process for managing FoI requests that is set out in Chapter 2 can be used to manage EIR requests. Unlike data protection, they are a straightforward request for information. There is a UK and a Scottish set of regulations, although these are very similar. Any differences between the two Regulations will be noted as necessary. Being a set of Regulations rather than an Act, the terminology is Regulation rather than section when referring to the separate parts of the Environmental Information Regulations (EIR), that is Regulation 1(1) rather than section 1(1).

As is expected from the name, the EIR focus on environmental information, as compared to FoI, which covers information more generally. Which leads to the first question when it comes to using the EIR: what is environmental information? The next section takes you through the definitions in the Regulations and how they can be used to identify environmental information.

Environmental information

Both Regulations take their definitions of environmental information directly from Directive 2003/4/EC, Public Access to Environmental Information, (referred to as 'the Directive' in this chapter) which was in turn drafted to meet the requirements of the Aarhus Convention.[1] The purpose of the Directive and the Regulations is to allow EU citizens access to environmental information in order to be able to participate in decision making relating to the environment.

In Regulation 2(1) for both the UK and Scottish Regulations, environmental information is defined in the following way:

> 'environmental information' has the same meaning as in Article 2(1) of the Directive,[2] namely any information in written, visual, aural, electronic or any other material form on—
>
> (a) the state of the elements of the environment, such as air and atmosphere, water, soil, land, landscape and natural sites including wetlands, coastal and marine areas, biological diversity and its components, including genetically modified organisms, and the interaction among these elements;
>
> (b) factors, such as substances, energy, noise, radiation or waste, including radioactive waste, emissions, discharges and other releases into the environment, affecting or likely to affect the elements of the environment referred to in (a);
>
> (c) measures (including administrative measures), such as policies, legislation, plans, programmes, environmental agreements, and activities affecting or likely to affect the elements and factors referred to in (a) and (b) as well as measures or activities designed to protect those elements;
>
> (d) reports on the implementation of environmental legislation;
>
> (e) cost-benefit and other economic analyses and assumptions used within the framework of the measures and activities referred to in (c); and
>
> (f) the state of human health and safety, including the contamination of the food chain, where relevant, conditions of human life, cultural sites and built structures inasmuch as they are or may be affected by the state of the elements of the environment referred to in (a) or, through those elements, by any of the matters referred to in (b) and (c).

The likelihood is that if the information can be tied to the environment in some way, it will fit within one or more of the definitions above. This means that if your organization has a focus on the environment, you will need to get to know the EIR well. However, other organizations will need to know the EIR for requests related to estates or building management departments, as it is likely that the information they hold will fit within the definition, whether this is obviously relating to the environment, for example 'the amount of emissions from an incinerator' or appears, for example, to be financial, such as 'how much did you spend on electricity last year?' If the information connects to the environment in any way, the request should be treated as an EIR request, not a FoI request.

Regulation 2(1)(a): the state of the elements of the environment

This covers all the items mentioned within the Regulation, but is not intended to cover only these elements, hence the use of 'such as'. This covers information about an element such as the state of a river or a wetland and also how these interact, for example, soil erosion due to exposure to wind.

As such, the definition includes the following:

- Air can refer to air samples confined outside the atmosphere as well as to air quality within the atmosphere.
- It does not matter where water is, so any body of water is covered, as well as samples from those bodies.
- Soil refers to the top layer of dirt used to grow plants, etc.
- Land covers both the surface and underground solid parts of the earth.[3]
- Landscapes and natural sites are similar but not the same. A landscape is more likely to be the result of human intervention and has a human viewpoint. Natural sites are more the creation of non-human species interacting with each other to create a specific type of environment like a wetland. Natural sites can exist without human intervention although they may have some human management. They do not have to be a Site of Special Scientific Interest to fit the definition.[4]
- Biological diversity covers how different species interact to keep

in balance. The ICO guidance states that it does not believe this covers a specific species studied in isolation,[5] but it will cover that species interacting with its environment or with another species in its natural environment, for example, a fungus grown in a laboratory on agar would not be covered, while the same fungus growing on a tree in a forest would be.

Regulation 2(1)(b): factors affecting the elements of the environment

Information that fits within this Regulation involves factors that affect the elements listed in 2(1)(a). As with the previous Regulation, the list of factors listed is not meant to be exhaustive. A factor includes something that has a physical effect on the elements of the environment, for example, waste being discharged into a river.[6] The effect should already have happened but could have stopped or still be ongoing.

As such, the definition includes the following:

- The effect can be positive or negative.
- A substance is physical matter in any form – so, gases, liquids and solids.
- Energy means heating and cooling generally, and specific forms of energy like wind or nuclear power. Technically, it also covers noise (sound energy) and radioactivity, although these are listed separately.
- Waste is anything that is no longer useful. Radioactive waste is a subcategory of this but obviously has its own issues.
- Emissions, discharges and releases covers any releases, deliberate or otherwise, into the environment. This covers energy and noise as well as substances.
- Regulation 5(5) also requires public authorities to provide on request how factors have been measured, by either a specific procedure or a standardised one.

Regulation 2(1)(c): measures and activities related to the environment

Information about policies, procedures, plans, etc. relating to the environment and activities like building work fit within this Regulation. The measures and activities have to be affecting or likely to affect the elements listed in Regulation 2(1)(a) and/or the factors listed in Regulation 2(1)(b). The effect of the measures and activities does not have to be large and could cover future plans as well as ongoing measures and activities.

Included within the definition are the following:

- Whether a proposed measure or activity actually comes to pass is not important. If it could affect the environment, it still counts under this Regulation.
- This Regulation in particular helps to support the general public in getting involved in plans relating to the environment. The public interest in releasing this type of information will always be very strong.
- The information covered by this Regulation will not just include policies and procedures but also the steps taken to implement them. The policies, etc. do not have to be directly about the environment, but do have to have an environmental impact.

> Whether information relating to a sub activity within a larger activity is covered was discussed in *Mersey Tunnel Users Association (MTUA) v Information Commissioner and Halton Borough Council.*[7] If the sub activity is integral to a measure or activity relating to the environment, then it is considered to fit within the scope of this Regulation. In this case, the fact that tolls (financial information) were proposed for an existing and a proposed bridge, the building of which would affect the environment, and that the bridge could not be built without the money raised by tolls meant that the report relating to charging tolls was considered by the Information Tribunal to be environmental information.[8]

Regulation 2(1)(d): reports on the implementation of environmental legislation

This regulation is fairly straightforward as it will cover any reports relating to environmental legislation and how it has been implemented.

There may be some overlap between the policies, procedures, plans, etc. covered by Regulation 2(1)(c) and the reports covered by this Regulation. Either way, they will all fit within the definition of environmental information.

Regulation 2(1)(e): economic analyses relating to information listed in Regulation 2(1)(c)

Again, this is fairly straightforward as shown in the MTUA judgement mentioned above. Any cost–benefit and/or other economic analyses that relate to environmental measures and activities are covered. The economic analyses have to relate to measures and analyses covered by Regulation 2(1)(c).

Regulation 2(1)(f): the state of human health and safety and conditions of human life

This Regulation has an obvious connection to health and safety, so it would cover information about contamination in the food chain. However, it has a wider meaning by including conditions of human life. As such, it covers the built environment created by humans and cultural sites if these relate to the state of the environment or factors, measures and activities relating to the environment.

When deciding if information fits this part of the definition of environmental information, think about the following:

- Human health and safety specifically includes contamination of the food chain. As an example, this shows the focus on collective health and safety rather than individual health and safety. The emphasis is on the environmental impact on humans rather than an individual risk like a trip hazard.
- Conditions of human life covers information relating to housing, access to clean water and health care, amongst other things, as long as these relate to the state of the environment. For example, information relating to drought conditions causing famine could be covered.
- The built environment and cultural sites are included where there is an environmental impact. For example, the plans relating to the

changes to the roads around Stonehenge could include information relating to the environmental impact on a cultural site, so they could be included within this Regulation.
- Although pylons and aerials are considered to be part of the built environment, the electrical and other emissions from them are covered by Regulation 2(1)(b).
- The ICO also lists planning decisions, property searches and listed building status as environmental information, due to the fact that these include alterations to the built environment or restrictions as to what can be done with the built environment. However, internal restructuring does not have an environmental impact, so it is not covered, although the waste from it may be.

Documents and records covering both environmental and non-environmental information

There may be cases where documents and records contain both environmental and non-environmental information. Technically this means that the EIR apply to the former and FoI to the latter.

> Whether this requires doing a line-by-line analysis was discussed in the *Department for Business, Enterprise and Regulatory Reform v Information Commissioner and Friends of the Earth*.[9] The Information Tribunal took a pragmatic approach by stating that 'we find that where the predominant purpose of the document covers environmental information then it may be possible to find that the whole document is subject to EIR. Where there are a number of purposes and none of them are dominant then it would appear that the public authority has no choice but to review the contents of the document in detail.'[10]

If you have a mixed request, you need to consider the following:

- Both FoI and the EIR are about access to information. So, if you are disclosing the information it really does not matter if you are using the FoI or EIR to release it, unless you want to do some awareness raising that the EIR exist.
- The differences come into play only when the information is being withheld. If it could be argued that a document broadly fits within

the definition of environmental information, you could argue that only the EIR exceptions apply. If it is more mixed, you may have to do a line-by-line analysis.

- Why did both the UK and Scottish governments go for two separate pieces of legislation, leaving us with these decisions? Because the EIR require more openness and there was certain information that was felt to need more protection than one piece of legislation based on the Directive could offer. As such, if you have information that you legitimately think is outside the scope of Regulation 2(1) and you want to exempt it from release, it will be worth your while to do the line-by-line analysis so that you can apply the FoI exemptions.

Who is covered by the EIR?

How do you know if you are covered by the EIR?

As stated within Regulation 3,[11] both the UK and Scottish Regulations cover public authorities, except for those acting in a judicial or legislative capacity. The UK EIR also state that the Houses of Parliament are not covered if it would infringe their privileges, and deliberately remove Scottish public authorities from the scope of the Regulations. Both cover what a (Scottish) public authority is in the definitions sections of their respective Regulation 2.[12]

All public authorities covered by FoI are also covered by the EIR. However, other organizations are also covered by the Regulations. However, aside from the organizations that you would expect to be covered, both sets of Regulations bring in other bodies that have a public administration function or public responsibilities related to the environment. This has mainly been done to ensure that utilities and other once-public sector organizations with an impact on the environment are included within the scope of the Regulations, to ensure that information relating to that impact can be made available to the general public.

The two Regulations differ in the way in which they bring such organizations within scope. The UK Regulations state the following:

> 'public authority' means—
> (a) government departments;

(b) any other public authority as defined in section 3(1) of the Act, disregarding for this purpose the exceptions in paragraph 6 of Schedule 1 to the Act, but excluding—
  (i) any body or office-holder listed in Schedule 1 to the Act only in relation to information of a specified description; or
  (ii) any person designated by Order under section 5 of the Act;
(c) any other body or other person, that carries out functions of public administration; or
(d) any other body or other person, that is under the control of a person falling within sub-paragraphs (a), (b) or (c) and—
  (i) has public responsibilities relating to the environment;
  (ii) exercises functions of a public nature relating to the environment; or
  (iii) provides public services relating to the environment.

Whereas the Scottish equivalent is:

'Scottish public authority' means –
(a) any body which, any other person who, or the holder of any office which is–
  (i) listed in schedule 1 to the Act (but subject to any qualification in that schedule), or
  (ii) designated by order under section 5(1) of the Act;
(b) a publicly-owned company as defined by section 6 of the Act;
(c) any other Scottish public authority with mixed functions or no reserved functions (within the meaning of the Scotland Act 1998(3)); and
(d) any other person who is neither a public body nor the holder of a public office and who is under the control of a person or body falling within paragraphs (a), (b) or (c) of this definition and–
  (i) has public responsibilities relating to the environment;
  (ii) exercises functions of a public nature relating to the environment; or
  (iii) provides public services relating to the environment.

So, to summarise, if you are covered by FoI, you are covered by the EIR. The exceptions for public authorities are as follows:

- Some public authorities outside the scope of FoI are included within the EIR, for example, special forces.
- If the organization is only partially covered by FoI, it is not included within the scope of the EIR. For example, the BBC, for which information relating to journalism, art or literature is out of scope in FoI, is not covered by the EIR.
- Any organization declared to be a public authority under section 5 of the FoIA or FoISA does not automatically become covered by the comparable EIR.
- While the Scottish EIR specifically mention wholly owned companies, these are covered by the UK Regulations as well, as they are within the scope of the FoIA.
- Scottish public authorities with mixed functions, that is, functions that derive from both Scottish and UK law, will be covered by one set of Regulations or the other.

This leaves the definitions in (c) for the UK EIR and (d) for both Regulations, which brings into scope other organizations which normally are private bodies with public functions relating to the environment. The FishLegal[13] case looked in depth into the definition of carrying out 'functions of public administration' for water companies. The Proceedings and their History in 1. Preliminary Matters states 'This is complicated', but if you are unsure if you are covered by the EIR it is worth reading this case in full, particularly the section discussing how the water companies were found to be public authorities. The Upper Tribunal focused on what powers the water companies had that a purely private company would not have. The examples provided in discussing the case included compulsory purchase, access to land without an owner's permission with the possibility of prosecuting criminal offences, for example, when enforcing a hosepipe ban,[14] and being subject to judicial review. The ICO also points to powers to advise a public authority, which brought the Verderers of the Forest of Dean within the scope of the Regulations.[15]

It could be that the special powers of your organization are not amongst those listed here, but if you are legally entitled to perform a function that a normal private company would not and information relating to that function could fit within the definition of environmental information, it could bring you within the scope of the Regulations.

The definition in (d) covers private organizations which could be said to be under the control of a public authority and which have a public role relating to the environment. Control would extend to being a majority shareholder, being able to make or annul decisions, being able to appoint or remove a managing board or to withdraw funding.[16]

> While there have been no decisions in the UK that have included organizations within this definition, in Scotland, the SIC found that a registered social landlord, Dunbritton, was under the control of the Scottish Housing Regulator as the latter had 'extensive powers of intervention in situations of alleged misconduct, mismanagement or underperformance and its powers to require remedial action'[17] in relation to Dunbritton. As a housing association, Dunbritton had powers relating to
>
> > construction of new social housing, improvements made to existing housing structure and the repair and planned maintenance of existing housing [which] can have significant effects on energy use. Energy is a factor included in regulation 2(1)(b) (definition of 'environmental information') of the EIRs; reducing energy use in housing can have a positive effect in reducing carbon dioxide emissions and therefore the state of the air and atmosphere.[18]
>
> As such, it was a Scottish public authority for the purposes of the Scottish Regulations.

And finally, if you are not covered by FoI but do have special powers in relation to the environment or are under the control of a public authority and hold information relating to the environment, you could be covered by the EIR.

So, in final summary, you are covered by the EIR if:

1 you are a public authority, unless excepted as shown above;
2 you are a wholly owned company of a public authority;
3 you have functions that come from legislation;
4 you are under the control of a public authority.

Processing EIR requests

You can easily log FoI and EIR requests on the one system by including a data field that allows you to indicate whether the request is covered by FoI or EIR or both. The same process of:

- identifying a request;
- logging a request;
- sending a request out to colleagues who hold the information;
- managing requests for clarification;
- sending reminders of the deadline to colleagues;
- drafting the response, including providing arguments for exceptions;
- obtaining sign-off;
- sending out the request;
- dealing with any complaints

occurs regardless of whether you are processing an FoI request or an EIR request. So it makes sense to log them both in the same place, rather than using two separate systems. The only extra thing you may have to do with EIR requests is to let colleagues know that the EIR apply rather than FoI, particularly if there is information that needs to be excepted from release.

Verbal requests

One of the main differences between the FoIAs and the EIR is that requests can be made verbally. Technically, a request could be made to any individual working at the public authority, with the expectation that the request will be responded to within 20 working days. In practice, the vast majority of requests for environmental information are made via e-mail, as for FoI requests. However, any guidance on the EIR that you issue to staff should include that the requests can be made verbally, so that they are aware of the possibility.

It is also good practice if you receive a verbal request to write down what you think has been requested and relay this back to the requester for checking. There is less likelihood of mistakes in supplying the information if it is written down and agreed. This would fit with the Regulation 9 duty to advise and assist. As with FoI requests, you want to make sure that you are actually providing the information requested, so writing down a verbal request and checking with the requester that this is correct is the starting point for ensuring that you are providing the correct information.

Time to respond

Normally, you have 20 working days to respond, as per FoI. However, Regulation 7 in both sets of Regulations allows for an extension to 40 working days if 'the complexity and volume of the information requested means that it is impracticable either to comply with the request within the earlier period or to make a decision to refuse to do so'.[19] This extension includes:

- supplying the information;
- explaining why you are not supplying the information in the format requested;
- explaining why you are refusing to supply the information.

So, to calculate the response date you need to consider the following:

- The complexity and volume of the information are the key points here. If you cannot provide the information within 20 working days or make a decision about whether to refuse to supply it, Regulation 7 could apply. However, if you think that you can supply it but it would just take longer, particularly if it is in the public interest to release the information, you can take the full 40 days.
- You must communicate the decision to use a further 20 working days within the first 20 working days.

Clarification, transfers and formats

As for FoI, you can request clarification if a request is unclear or too broad. Regulation 9 in both sets of Regulations is the equivalent of the FoI duty to advise and assist, so if you are refusing a request because it is too broad, you do have to communicate with the requester to find out exactly what it is they want from what you can provide.

Also, as for FoI, if you do not hold the information but know the public authority that does, you should consider either supplying the requester with the contact details of the organization or transferring the request directly to it.[20] If you are in some way connected to the other public authority but it is not clear why it would hold the information and why you do not, you are encouraged by the Code of Practice[21] to inform the requester of the difference.

Requesters can also specify the formats in which they want the information, which should be complied with unless you have a good reason not to provide it, as set out in Regulation 6 in both sets of Regulations. That is, do not provide in hardcopy or PDF what you hold in a spreadsheet, i.e. as a .csv file. The .csv file is easier to manipulate if the requester plans on reusing it. If, however, you hold the information only in hardcopy, you can refuse to transfer it to an electronic form.

If you are providing information in a reusable format, the Re-use of Public Sector Information (RPSI) Regulations could apply. So, if the requester has indicated that they intend to reuse the information it would be worth supplying the licence relating to the information and any fees that you might charge for re-use, although these have to be reasonable. The RPSI Regulations are covered in more detail in Chapter 8.

Charging fees

A public authority is entitled to charge a reasonable amount for environmental information.[22] What a reasonable amount can include was decided at the European Court of Justice (CJEU) in *East Sussex County Council v Information Commissioner*.[23] The original request concerned information held on a database. East Sussex County Council argued that the charge covered both responding to the requests for information and maintaining the database that held the information. CJEU judged that only activities involved in responding to requests were covered and that maintaining the database was not within scope.[24]

So, a reasonable amount would cover staff time in responding to the request and disbursements like printing and postage, etc. that relate to the request. However, the fee cannot include activities that maintain the information, for example, staff costs relating to maintaining a database. The ICO states that it believes it is more reasonable to charge for staff time and materials where there is an obvious connection to processing the request, so you will definitely be able to include the price of paper. If there are several elements to the fee, you can provide a schedule to the requester.

If you are a self-supporting public authority, particularly one that competes in the market-place by providing information, a reasonable fee may be larger than for a one-off request at another public authority.

As for FoI, a public authority can require that the fee is paid before providing the information. However, the fee cannot be so large that it acts as an obstacle to the requester getting the information requested. If there is a large amount of information that needs processing, which would lead to a high fee, it is better to refuse the request as manifestly unreasonable (see below).

You cannot charge a fee for viewing public registers and lists of environmental information or for viewing environmental information *in situ*.

A public authority should have a schedule of its fees publicly available as per Regulation 8(8), which also requires a public authority to state when it would charge or waive any fees. If you are not certain how to present this, there are several good examples on local authority websites, for example, https://www.basingstoke.gov.uk/FOIfees,[25] that cover both FoI and EIR fees.

Exceptions: EIR-speak for exemptions

While the presumption with the EIR is that information will be released, there are exceptions. Some of these are similar to FoI exemptions – for example, the exception for personal data. However, some are particular to the EIR and all are subject to the public interest test. There are no absolute exceptions under the EIR. The exceptions are found in Regulation 12 of the UK Regulations and Regulation 10 of the Scottish Regulations, although both have a separate Regulation for personal data (Regulations 13 and 11, respectively).

The refusal notice for an EIR request will have to include a public interest test. Do not be tempted to try to refuse using an FoI exemption – if the information fits within the definition of environmental information, you must apply the EIR exceptions instead. The ICO/SIC will strike out any FoI exemptions you attempt to use and require you to find the relevant EIR exception. This is why it is important to be certain that the information fits the definition of environmental information right from the start.

Regulation 12(4)/10(4): the 'administrative' or class-based exceptions

The exceptions in this regulation cover situations which are administrative in nature, rather than related to specific information. The text for both regulations is virtually the same:

> a public authority may refuse to disclose information to the extent that—
> (a) it does not hold that information when an applicant's request is received;
> (b) the request for information is manifestly unreasonable;
> (c) the request for information is formulated in too general a manner and the public authority has complied with regulation 9;
> (d) the request relates to material which is still in the course of completion, to unfinished documents or to incomplete data; or
> (e) the request involves the disclosure of internal communications.[26]

As with all the exceptions, the public interest test applies and must be conducted when deciding on whether to use the exception or not.

Regulation 12(4)(a)/10(4)(a): information not held

As for FoI, information not held can be subject to interpretation. If you simply do not have the information on your systems and no reason to record it, this is a straightforward exception. If the information is held within systems but not precisely in the way requested, the decision on whether you hold it becomes less certain. If you can extract the information within the time limit for the response, even if it means creating a new query to extract the data, then you would be considered to hold it.

It will be hard to apply the public interest test where you simply do not hold the information. However, whether there is a public interest in extracting information that would meet the request should be a factor in deciding whether to create a new query is necessary.

As with FoI, if you know who does hold the information, you will have to transfer the request by following Regulation 10/3 regarding transfer.

Regulation 12(4)(b)/10(4)(b): manifestly unreasonable

This exception covers the same situations in FoI relating to vexatious requests or requests that breach the cost limit. The focus on applying this exception is on whether it will disrupt the work of the public authority, whether it has a malicious intent and whether it will simply cost too much for the public authority to comply with it. Unlike the FoI Acts, you do have to consider the public interest even if the request is vexatious or too expensive to process. However, the ICO does not consider it a duty to advise and assist if the request fits within the vexatious category for this exception.[27]

> That the same tests for vexatious apply to similar requests refused under this exception was discussed by the Upper Tribunal in *Craven v Information Commissioner and Department of Environment and Climate Change*.[28] After deciding that not much clarification was available via the definitions within the Aarhus Convention and the Directive, it was the phrase 'misuse of rights' that was raised in a case heard by the European Court of Justice[29] that was found to be closest to defining manifestly unreasonable. This was decided to be equivalent to the 'abuse of process'[30] raised in the Dransfield[31] decision.

Where complying with a request could not be done within even the 40 day extension provided in Regulation 7, this exception can also apply. However, there is no equivalent to the cost limit in FoI. The ICO provides four different tests to determine if a request will be too burdensome to respond to:

- the nature of the request and any wider value in the requested information being made publicly available;
- the importance of any underlying issue to which the request relates, and the extent to which responding to the request would illuminate that issue;
- the size of the public authority and the resources available to it, including the extent to which the public authority would be distracted from delivering other services; and

- the context in which the request is made, which may include the burden of responding to other requests on the same subject from the same requester.[32]

It is likely to be harder to argue costs for EIR requests unless you can meet all of these tests. A request for information relating to a live issue or one with great impact on the environment – for example, a discharge of waste into a river that is still being cleaned up – will be less likely to be considered manifestly unreasonable even if the amount of information is large and complex to process. You will be required to provide good cost estimates relating to processing the request, and while the regulators will have the cost limits in FoI in mind, the presumption of release in the EIR means that they will not apply them to EIR requests as a matter of principle.

You are more likely to be able to apply this exception to multiple similar requests for information,[33] where the requester appears to have a monomania about an issue or where it is obvious that you simply do not have the resources to meet the request. For example, a parish council is more likely to meet the requirements of the tests above than a large government department. If complying with the request(s) would disrupt a public authority's ability to do their other work, then it is more likely to meet the manifestly unreasonable test.

Regulation 12(4)(c)/10(4)(c): request is too general

If you cannot understand what is being requested or the request is too broad, you can refuse the request using this exception. You do have to have first provided advice and assistance under Regulation 9. As such, if the request can be interpreted in two or more ways and you are not certain which applies, or if you can provide a subset of information, you need to communicate this to the requester. If they confirm the interpretation or agree to a narrower request, you should process the request as normal. If they do not confirm a particular interpretation or insist on the original request being complied with, then you can apply this exception, provided that it is in the public interest to do so.

When applying this exception you need to think about the following:

- A request referring to, for example, 'a river' rather than a specific river could fall within this exception.
- Like Regulation 12(4)(a)/10(4)(a), this will be difficult to apply the public interest test to, as it relates to not understanding what the request is for.

Regulation 12(4)(d)/10(4)(d): unfinished or incomplete information

This exception covers three classes of information: material which is still in the course of completion, unfinished documents and incomplete data. The sort of information that could be included within the scope of the exception is:

- information relating to a project that is currently being prepared or in draft form. This does not include finished documents relating to a project. If some of the project documentation is complete even if the project itself is not, the complete project documents are not covered by the exception;
- a draft report for which a final report has been released;[34]
- data which is still being collected and is not being used in its incomplete form by a public authority. If the incomplete dataset is being used, this exception no longer applies.

The public interest test for this exception will need careful balancing between the need for public authorities to consider options relating to the environment and the right of the public to know about decisions relating to the environment. The draft report listed above may still be in the public interest to release if it either is not too different from the final report or shows a major difference to the final report in that the public authority made changes to the report on account of new environmental duties.

Regulation 12(4)(e)/10(4)(e): internal communications

This potentially covers a wide range of information exchanged within a public authority. However, there is a strong presumption towards disclosure and the public interest test is likely to conclude that information should be released. The exception will apply if there is a strong indication that release would harm decision making relating to the environment. However, unlike Regulation 12(4)(d)/10(4)(d), this exception can apply to finished documentation.

Internal communications infers that the information has been communicated internally. That is, it cannot relate to information created by a single staff member that has not been circulated to other staff. It also does not include information that was circulated both internally and externally. If an e-mail chain is partially circulated externally, that part will not fall within the exception but a branch of the chain only circulated internally will.

'Internal' can include related public authorities. The example given by the SIC is the Radioactive Waste Advisory Committee, which has a direct reporting role to the Scottish Government.[35] Central government departments are also considered one public authority for the purposes of this exception.[36] However, communications between UK government departments and the devolved assemblies are not considered internal.[37] For communications to be internal between two public authorities, there has to be a direct reporting relationship. External advisers will normally not be considered to be internal, but it is possible[38] if the relationship is close enough. If the information has gone to a third party that is not another public authority with a direct reporting relationship to yours, this exception does not apply.

The public interest test for this exception will focus on whether the information allows the public authority to maintain a private thinking space. As with arguments relating to safe spaces and the chilling effect, it will need to be argued how release of the internal communications could stop a decision-making process or exchange of views from occurring. So, while a wide range of unfinished and finished documentation could be covered, the public interest test is going to be a high hurdle for this exception. You will need to provide good arguments as to why decision making or frank exchange of views will be harmed by release of the information.

Regulation 12(5)/10(5): the subject-based exceptions

Unlike the previous regulation, this regulation applies to

information to the extent that its disclosure would adversely affect—

(a) international relations, defence, national security or public safety;
(b) the course of justice, the ability of a person to receive a fair trial or the ability of a public authority to conduct an inquiry of a criminal or disciplinary nature;
(c) intellectual property rights;
(d) the confidentiality of the proceedings of that or any other public authority where such confidentiality is provided by law;
(e) the confidentiality of commercial or industrial information where such confidentiality is provided by law to protect a legitimate economic interest;
(f) the interests of the person who provided the information where that person—
    (i) was not under, and could not have been put under, any legal obligation to supply it to that or any other public authority;
    (ii) did not supply it in circumstances such that that or any other public authority is entitled apart from these Regulations to disclose it; and
    (iii) has not consented to its disclosure; or
(g) the protection of the environment to which the information relates.[39]

'Adversely affect' is taken to mean 'harm'. In this way, it works very similarly to the prejudice test in FoI. You will need to show harm to the interests within the exceptions.

> This was discussed in *Archer v Information Commissioner's Office*, and the steps laid out in that case for determining if interests will be adversely affected are very useful to consider:
>
> > First, it is not enough that disclosure should simply affect the matters set out in paragraph 50 above; the effect must be "adverse". Second, refusal to disclose is only permitted to the extent of that adverse effect. Third, it is necessary to show that disclosure "would" have an adverse effect – not that it could or might have such effect. Fourth, even if there would be an adverse effect, the information must still be disclosed unless "in all the circumstances of the case, the public interest in maintaining the exception outweighs the public interest in disclosing the information". All these issues must be assessed having regard to the overriding presumption in favour of disclosure.[40]

The public interest test then needs to be carried out, as for the Regulation 12(4)/10(4) exceptions. Keeping the presumption towards disclosure in mind, this means that while you may have exceptions that do not have equivalent exemptions, like intellectual property, they are harder to use.

So to apply these exceptions, you will need to focus on the following:

- The interests in the exception must be harmed by release, not simply affected.
- The information being excepted must relate specifically to the harm. You cannot use these exceptions in a blanket way.
- You will still have to conduct a public interest test, even if harm could occur.
- A statutory bar creates an absolute exemption for FoI in the UK, but will be only one factor in a public interest test.
- Private interests are not the same as public interests. Information that could be useful in only one individual case may be more likely to be excepted than information that affects the public more generally.
- Only the first three exceptions can be used for information relating to emissions.

Regulation 12(5)(a)/10(5)(a): international relations, defence, national security or public safety

This exception groups together adverse effects to international relations, defence, national security and public safety. Most of these are also covered by FoI exemptions, so you will have to consider the exception when environmental information intersects with these interests. This is the only exception to allow for neither confirm nor deny if to do so would also adversely affect the interests in this exception.

International relations covers environmental information relating to relations between states or in international organizations. It is likely to cover information which would weaken the UK's bargaining position or damage relations with another state or international organization. Even if information does fall into this category, for example, weather data collected from the equivalent of the Met Office all over the world, you still must focus on the harm. The University of East Anglia was unable to prove that weather stations would stop providing weather data if they knew that it could be released under the EIR in the UK.[41]

Defence will cover environmental information that relates to the armed forces and defence of the UK, so it could cover the environmental impact of the armed forces. The focus of the exception would therefore be on whether releasing the information would harm the ability of the armed forces to function. National security will cover military defence, but also protection of democracy and the legal system.[42] This has been successfully used by Ofcom to except information relating to mobile phone tower bases, on the basis that knowing exactly where these are would make them more open to attack and theft.[43]

Also, remember that public safety is seen by the ICO as similar to protecting health and safety.

Regulation 12(5)(b)/10(5)(b): course of justice

This exception is the equivalent to legal professional privilege in FoI, although it also covers law enforcement investigations and proceedings and records relating to courts, tribunals and inquiries.

As with FoI, legal professional privilege is considered to be strongest while a case is live. If the information is to be used for a pending court case relating to the environment, it is more likely to engage the exception than once the case is finished. Court records or related records will be more likely to be excepted if they refer to a live or pending case. This was confirmed by the Information Tribunal in *Watts v the Information Commissioner*.[44]

The ICO considers that as the 'course of justice' is fairly broad, information labelled 'without prejudice' may also be covered by this exception. However, this has not been confirmed yet by the Information Tribunal.[45] However, it is likely that information that could be used in law enforcement or other proceedings, even if the investigation has ended, may be covered by this exception if further information could re-open the case.

Regulation 12(5)(c)/10(5)(c): intellectual property rights

This is the one point where intellectual property is explicitly dealt with in an information rights law. The ICO states that of all the intellectual property rights available, the ones most likely to interact with this exception are copyright, database rights and copyright in databases.[46] In deciding if this exception applies, the harm will have to be to someone's rights relating to their intellectual property. The harm will not relate to release itself under the Regulations, as there is an exemption in the Copyright, Designs and Patents Act relating to the release of information required by statute.[47] Regulation 5(6) also states that there is no legislation that can stop information being released under the Regulations. The harm must relate to what use the requester may make of the information and whether this would infringe on intellectual property rights.

To use this exception, you must think about the following:

- You will need to identify both who holds the intellectual property rights and what specific right is being harmed.
- A public authority will hold copyright in information it produces, although this could also be covered by Crown or Parliamentary copyright. However, information provided by third parties to a public authority is likely to be the property of the third party.
- Database rights apply only when a public authority or third party has put substantial work into creating and maintaining a database.
- Copyright in databases is not in the individual records, but in the decisions on how to arrange the database.
- Harm does not just mean that intellectual property rights are infringed. There must be actual or potential loss or damage to the rights holder. If a third party is the intellectual property owner, they must be consulted as to what the damage could be.
- Commercial losses are covered by Regulation 12(5)(e)/10(5)(e) and it would be worth considering both exceptions to see which fits best.

Regulation 12(5)(d)/10(5)(d): confidentiality in proceedings

The adverse effect here is to proceedings which have legal confidentiality. Proceedings are likely to be covered if there is a statutory or other legal reason for keeping them confidential. For example, records relating to a Council meeting where a particular section of the meeting is closed to discuss confidential matters could be covered by this exception.[48]

Things to consider are the following:

- Other legal reasons could include the common law definition of confidentiality. There does not have to be a statute that applies.

Regulation 12(5)(e)/10(5)(e): commercial-in-confidence information

There is a four-step test for applying this exception set out by the Information Tribunal in *Bristol City Council v Information Commissioner and Portland and Brunswick Squares Association*.[49] The tests are as follows.

1 The information is commercial or industrial in nature.
2 Confidentiality is provided by law.
3 The confidentiality is protecting a legitimate economic interest.
4 The confidentiality would be adversely affected by disclosure.

Things to consider are the following:

- Due to the confidentiality needing to be provided by law, this is not comparable with the commercial-in-confidence exemption in FoI.
- Trade secrets are definitely covered by the exception, unless they relate to emissions.
- Commercial does not equal financial. There must be a trade of some sort for the exception to apply. Industrial information will cover manufacture of goods generally, including raw materials.
- Although the test for confidentiality is similar to that in FoI, there does not have to be an actionable breach of confidence, just an expectation of confidentiality that has a legal basis.
- The ICO defines legitimate economic interests as 'retaining or improving market position, ensuring that competitors do not gain access to commercially valuable information, protecting a commercial bargaining position in the context of existing or future

negotiations, avoiding commercially significant reputational damage, or avoiding disclosures which would otherwise result in a loss of revenue or income'.[50]

Regulation 12(5)(f)/10(5)(f): personal interests

This exception does not cover personal information, which is covered below. It covers information provided by an individual who was under no obligation to provide it and who did not expect it to be released nor has agreed to its release.

Things to be considered are the following:

- This is likely to cover information provided by whistle blowers or people who are acting in a private capacity whose relationships with others could be harmed by release.
- It may also cover the deceased, whose personal information would no longer be covered by Data Protection law.

Regulation 12(5)(g)/10(5)(g): protection of the environment

This exception covers cases where release of information would cause harm to the environment rather than protecting it.

Things to be considered are the following:

- It's likely to be obvious when this exception applies, for example, if it relates to a rare bird's nesting site and letting people know about it could cause the nest to be disturbed.

Personal data and the EIR

Regulation 13 in the UK Regulations and Regulation 11 in the Scottish Regulations are the ones relating to personal data. Both work similarly to the FoI personal data exemptions in that neither of the Regulations can be used by a data subject for their personal data.[51] There are then further tests relating to third-party personal data, which are similar to those for FoI (see the section on section 40/38 in Chapter 3).

Complaints about EIR requests

These follow the same course as FoI requests. So, offer an internal review as shown in Chapter 3, which can be followed by the relevant Information Commissioner and then the courts.

Conclusion

Now that you have finished this chapter, you should know:

- how to recognise a request relating to environmental information;
- how to apply the exceptions in the Regulations.

For how to manage requests as per FoI, see Chapter 2.

8

Other information-related laws

Introduction

Aside from the big three information rights laws, there are other specific pieces of legislation that you may need to know about, depending on the sort of records you hold. The table below points you to the relevant sections of this chapter.

Records held/area of work	**Chapter section**
Medical records	Access to medical records
Local government	Access to local government records
Central government, local government, some other public bodies or a library, museum or archive in the public sector	Re-use of Public Sector Information Regulations
Using personal data for marketing purposes	Privacy and Electronic Communications Regulations and the ePrivacy Regulation
Information security	Computer Misuse Act
Covered by Crown Copyright or Freedom of Information	Public Records Act and the Code of Practice for Records Management
Public authority holding spatial datasets	INSPIRE Regulations

Access to medical records

Although the Data Protection legislation allows for access to an individual's medical records on the grounds that they are personal data, there is legislation in the UK that allows access to medical records for third parties in specific circumstances. If you work for or as a medical or health professional in the UK you will need to know about the following two Acts.

Access to Health Records Act 1990

This Act allows access to 'individuals [who] are defined under Section 3(1)(f) of that Act as, "the patient's personal representative and any person who may have a claim arising out of the patient's death". A personal representative is the executor or administrator of the deceased person's estate.'[1] Others with a claim, e.g. a financial claim on the deceased, may also be allowed access to the records, but this needs to be assessed at the time of the request. Requests must be responded to within 21 days if the record(s) were added in the last 40 days, or within 40 days otherwise. The health records must be held by a health professional, which has the same definition as in the DPA,[2] and the request must be made directly to the relevant health professional with enough description to help them to find the records.

Access to Medical Reports Act 1988

This Act[3] covers reports made by a medical practitioner for the purposes of employment and/or insurance. The medical practitioner receives the request from the patient, but sends it to the employer, the employer's occupational health provider and/or an insurer. The medical practitioner cannot pass it on to a third party without the patient's consent, unless 21 days have passed since the patient requested access but has made no further communications. The purpose of the Act is to allow patients to see and suggest changes before the report is sent to the employer or insurer. Medical practitioners can charge a fee for access. There are some exemptions to release, for example, if the medical practitioner believes it will cause harm for the report to be released to the patient.

Other countries also allow access to medical records; for example, Canada gives patients a right to see their records, confirmed by the Supreme Court, although a doctor retains the ownership of the records. The USA provides access to medical records through the

Health Insurance Portability Accountability Act, Title II, where access is granted to patients or their guardians when a fee has been paid. However, this exempts some records, like psychotherapy notes, from release and also allows transfer to third parties who pay for health care, like insurers. Australia follows a similar regime to Canada, with access provided but with ownership staying with the health practitioner. Public hospitals require a flat fee to be paid, while private hospitals set their own fees.

Health data can also be requested from NHS Digital, who, under the provisions of the Care Act 2014, are able to disseminate information for the purposes of '(a) the provision of health care or adult social care, or (b) the promotion of health'.[4]

Access to local government records

Aside from FoI, Data Protection and the EIR, other legislation covers access to local government records, which you will need to know about if you work in local government in the UK. The Local Government (Access to Information) Act 1985[5] amended the 1972 Local Government Act to allow access to committee meetings, agendas, minutes and connected reports, unless the business discussed was confidential.

The definition of confidential information in section 100A(3) of the amended 1972 Act is:

> (a) information furnished to the council by a Government department upon terms (however expressed) which forbid the disclosure of the information to the public; and
> (b) information the disclosure of which to the public is prohibited by or under any enactment or by the order of a court;
>
> and, in either case, the reference to the obligation of confidence is to be construed accordingly.

The amendment also requires:

- registers of council members and committee members;
- copies of the documents

to be provided on request, for which a fee can be charged.

Re-use of Public Sector Information Regulations

The Re-use of Public Sector Information (RPSI) Regulations[6] cover what a requester can do with public sector information when they receive it. That is, the Regulations allow for the use of the data for a commercial or other purpose like creating an app. As such, it generally comes into play after information is made available via FoI or an EIR request. Use of the RPSI Regulations is fairly rare, in that most people just use the information provided to them anyway, but you do need to be aware of them in case you get a request. They come from an EU Directive 2013/37/EU of the European Parliament and the Council of 26 June 2013 (the 2013 Directive) (O.J. No. L175/1, 27.6.2013), which amended the previous Directive 2003/98/EC on the re-use of public sector information (the 2003 Directive).

The purpose of the RPSI Regulations is to give a licence to a third party to reuse information produced for a public task by a public authority. Not all public authorities are covered by these Regulations, as not all are considered to have 'public tasks'. As such, central and local government are covered with other public bodies specified in Regulation 3. Outside the scope of the RPSI are educational bodies, public sector broadcasters and public sector performing arts organizations. However, all libraries, museums and archives are within scope, so university libraries, museums and archives are within scope while the rest of the university is not, which means that if you work for a university you will still need a working knowledge of these Regulations.

The RPSI Regulations are similar to FoI in that requests have to be made in writing and responded to within 20 working days. Recording requests under the RPSI could possibly be done by the use of additional fields where you record FoI and EIR requests, but recording them separately helps to keep track of deadlines. One major difference between FoI and the RPSI Regulations is that FoI is purpose blind, while requests under the RPSI Regulations have to include a description of the intended re-use.[7] Also, you can take longer than 20 days to decide on re-use but the extra time period has to be reasonable.

If you are a relevant public authority and have released information to a requester, you are likely to be required to make it available under the RPSI Regulations. However, if the information is exempt, it will be outside the scope of the Regulations, except for the following case. If it is already publicly available, and therefore covered by the exemptions in section 21 of the UK FoIA and section 25 of the FoISA, it should still be offered under licence for re-use.

While several licences are available, the recommended licence is the Open Government Licence (OGL). Once the OGL is said to apply to information, there is no need for a requester to register that they will reuse the information and no fee should be charged for reuse. The purpose of this is to make information as free and open to reuse as possible, although you can still ask for attribution. The National Archives provides a list of Copyright Notices on its website[8] to which you could direct requesters so that they can attribute the information correctly.

Fees for disbursements can be charged, but as per Regulation 15(6):

> The total charge shall not exceed the sum of—
> (a) direct costs;
> (b) a reasonable apportionment of indirect and overhead costs attributable to chargeable activity; and
> (c) a reasonable return on investment.

If a fee has been charged for copies of documents under FoI or the EIR, you cannot charge again for re-use.[9] A schedule of fees should be included in the IAR, which is a requirement of Regulation 16(7). An IAR lists the main documents and information available for re-use.

However, some exceptions are allowed for re-use of information, which either means that another licence can be used or the information can be refused a licence for re-use. The exceptions requiring other licences are:

- where information can be charged for re-use so needs a licence covering the charges, which is most likely for public authorities that are self-supporting. A template for a charged licence is available from The National Archives website.
- where information is fine for non-commercial use, but not necessarily commercial use and the public body has a delegation of authority from Her Majesty's Stationery Office (HMSO). The delegation of authority is supplied only if a business case shows that an OGL is not appropriate. Two separate licences are available:

  - a developer licence, which can be granted for 6–12 months to allow a developer to work with the data to see if there are commercially viable uses. This requires registration by the developer;
  - the non commercial government licence, which allows re-use of Crown Copyright material;
- the specific Open Supreme Court licence for re-use of the Supreme Court's information;
- military insignia, which are licensed by the Ministry of Defence directly;
- software code developed by a public authority, which can be released under an Open Source Initiative, particularly where this will provide a financial benefit to the taxpayer.

There are also outright exceptions for information which mean that those categories of information cannot be made available under an OGL. These are:

- personal data, which has to be treated in line with the DPA/GDPR, and so redacted or anonymised;
- where the information rights are held by a third party, including copyright, patents, trademarks and design rights;
- departmental logos, crests, military insignia and the Royal Arms, unless integral to a document or dataset.

Like FoI and the EIR, the complaints process relating to a decision to reuse data starts with an internal review and then the ICO. The ICO has made one decision relating to the RPSI Regulations, involving Cambridgeshire County Council.[10]

This involved a request for the re-use of right of way information that the Council restricted for one year and which the requester complained did not allow further re-use by third parties (downstream re-use). It did, however, waive the fee of £72 that it would otherwise charge. The Council did not respond to a request for internal review, even when ordered to do so by the ICO, so the ICO went to the next stage in the complaint process. The Council did not agree that it had ever restricted downstream re-use, although the licence agreement stated 'allowing End-users to use the Information as authorised by an End-user Licence (except that an End-user shall not have the right to sub-license the right to access the Information)'.[11] The argument that it made for the 1 year licence was that this kept data up to date and renewal was always possible. The requester argued that this limited re-use, as the data would be embedded in the maps and difficult to extract. The ICO instead ordered that the information be made available under the OGL, as the Council's restrictions were too limiting. This was particularly the case as most Councils had released such data under an open licence.

Privacy and Electronic Communications Regulations and the ePrivacy Regulation

The Privacy and Electronic Communications Regulations (PECR)[12] cover privacy from a more specific angle than Data Protection. PECR cover consent for marketing via telephone, e-mail, text messaging and fax as well as website cookies, security of public electronic communication services and the privacy of customers using those networks. So, if you market your services electronically, track users on your website using cookies and communication with the general public via electronic communication services, you need to know about these Regulations.

You will still need to have identified a condition for processing within the DPA or GDPR for processing any personal data that you have collected for contacting people. However, under DPA/GDPR this will not necessarily be consent. It is the PECR that will require you to obtain consent for marketing via electronic messaging. You will need to ensure that staff at your organization understand the difference.

The ICO defines electronic communications as 'any information sent between particular parties over a phone line or internet connection. This includes phone calls, faxes, text messages, video messages, e-mails and internet messaging. It does not include generally available information such as the content of web pages or broadcast programming.'[13] Paper communications are not included within this definition either. Marketing covers free events that your organization may offer as well as requests for donations or fundraising. Even if you are making an initial contact to see if someone would be interested in the future, you are covered by PECR for those communications. However, customer service types of communication are outside the scope of these Regulations, so a phone call to an individual about a problem with the service your organization provides is not covered by these Regulations. PECR covers unsolicited communications, that is, those that are not initiated by the individual themselves.

Consent has to be freely given by the individual. It is best practice to cover all forms of communication that you intend to use separately, so allow individuals to choose if they want to be contacted by e-mail, text, telephone, etc. rather than just a give general consent for contact by any means which your organization deems necessary. The consent should be granted by a positive action by the individual, for example, allowing them to tick a box. The ICO guidance is not to pre-tick a box which individuals have to untick – it is best practice to aim for opt in, rather than make people opt out. Like consent within the DPA/GDPR, consent can be withdrawn at any time, and once it has been withdrawn you cannot market to people via the methods for which you no longer have consent. You need to ensure that any third parties that you have used to market your organization are also complying with PECR.

Regarding telephone calls, you (and any third parties) also need to check that someone has not signed up to the Telephone Preference Service (TPS),[14] so that you do not include people who have expressly not consented to being contacted by telephone. You will need proof that people who are signed up to the TPS have agreed to you marketing your services to them by telephone. Regulations 19 and 21 cover automated and direct telephone calls, respectively. Automated calls are forbidden unless you have explicit consent for this type of marketing. Direct telephone calls can be made unless the individual concerned has not consented or is on the TPS or has previously said they do not want to be contacted. For both automated and direct calls, you must say who is calling and give individuals a telephone number (freephone) or a contact address. Businesses can also have the same rights relating to consent for telephone marketing, for example, sole traders and some partnerships where they are considered as individuals rather than businesses for the purpose of the Regulations. Marketing by fax works the same way, in that you will need to check the Fax Preference Service (FPS).

E-mail rules are slightly different in that you need consent for initial e-mail contact. However, existing customers can be treated differently. For these, you can send marketing e-mails for similar services and goods to those already purchased, as long as you allow an easy opt out to future communications within the e-mail. This also applies to text, voice or image messaging, but in all cases, both at the initial communication and any subsequent communications, the opt out has to be clear. Do not think that viral marketing gets around PECR. If your organization is the instigator of the message, even if you are using individuals to communicate to other individuals about your services or goods, you are covered by the Regulations.

The PECR is the reason why websites started giving cookie notices. Cookies are small text files that are downloaded on a device and track use of a website. The notices are required because Regulation 6 requires that your organization lets people know that a cookie will be downloaded, what it is for and to enable consent for downloading them, usually by providing a link or by closing the notice. Your organization should list on your website what cookies are used, and it is good practice to provide some instructions on how to disable them. Any type of surveillance file is covered by Regulation 6, which outlaws the use of spyware. There are some exemptions to obtaining consent if the cookie is required to provide a service via the website, but the ICO guidance is to still let people know that these are being used.

The security related regulations apply mostly to telecommunications and internet service providers, so they are unlikely to apply to most organizations. If you compile a directory of subscribers or users that you make available to the public, you will be covered by Regulation 18. You need to let those individuals know what information will be made available and give them a chance to opt out.

Computer Misuse Act

The Computer Misuse Act[15] creates specific offences for: unauthorised access to computer materials; intent to commit or facilitate commission of further offences; intent to impair or reckless impairment of the operation of a computer; causing or creating risk of serious damage; and making or providing articles for use in the offences listed above. While it is more likely that your organization's information security staff will have a better knowledge of this Act, it lends support to any actions that must be undertaken to secure personal data. It could also possibly be used for exempting information from release under FoI section 44, statutory bars to release of information, where release of information could be used to undermine your organization's information systems security.

Public Records Act and the Code of Practice for Records Management

Access to information legislation is only as useful as the underlying management of public sector information. There are several Acts and Regulations that cover how public authorities should manage records. Not all the Acts cover all public authorities, but the Code of Practice for Records Management required by section 46 of the FoIA does cover every public authority covered by FoI and the EIRs.[16] Section 61 of the FoISA performs the same function for Scottish public authorities.

The Public Records Act 1958[17] governs transfer of public records to The National Archives and other places of deposit. Not all public authorities are subject to the Public Records Act, although all central government departments are covered. The duties of public authorities covered by the Act include identification and transfer of public records to The National Archives or a place of deposit and disposal of all other records. A departmental records officer needs to be appointed to oversee this work. The Local Government (Records) Act 1962 and certain sections of the Local Government Act 1972 create similar obligations for local government records. Universities, schools and non-departmental public bodies whose supporting legislation does not make them subject to the Public Records Act are outside the scope of the Act.

FoIA section 46/FoISA section 61 required that the government produce a Code of Practice on Records Management, which sets out for all public authorities how they should manage their records. This is discussed in more detail in Chapter 9; in summary, it consists of two parts. The first part covers how records should be managed and the second covers transfer to places of deposit for those public authorities required to do so.

INSPIRE Regulations

If your public authority produces spatial datasets, it will be covered by these Regulations. There are both UK and Scottish versions of the INSPIRE Regulations,[18] which link to the EIR. The EU Directive responsible for these was introduced to set up a network for sharing spatial data, that is, data relating to specific geographic locations. Public authorities with spatial datasets must create specific metadata relating to the datasets which is made available to the general public via the data.gov.uk website. As with making information available under the EIR, your organization can charge for access to some datasets. The INSPIRE Regulations required the relevant public authorities to make datasets available by December 2013 and EU member states are required to report annually on the datasets available. The ICO oversees compliance with these Regulations.

Conclusion

Now that you have finished this chapter, you should know:

- what other legislation may allow people to make requests for information;
- how to handle access to medical records;
- how to handle access to local government records;
- how to handle requests for re-use of information;
- what consents you need to gain to use marketing data;
- how the computer misuse act interacts with information rights legislation;
- how the Public Records Act and section 46 Code of Practice support information rights law;
- how to handle requests for spatial datasets.

For guidance on recording requests, see Chapter 2. While this is focused on FoI, you can manage requests under the other legislation in a similar fashion.

For how to manage the record-keeping requirements that underpin the rights to information, see Chapter 9.

9

Fitting information and records management into information rights work

Introduction

It is usual that you will also be managing records as well as responding to requests for information, particularly in organizations that are not big enough to require an information governance team. One-man bands covering information rights and information and records management (IRM) are common. The issues relating to this are:

1 convincing staff in your organization to properly manage their records in order to support providing information in response to requests;
2 applying records management principles so as to, at best, help support staff in their daily work and, at least, avoid a practice recommendation from the Information Commissioner;
3 finding the time for IRM tasks that don't have the same tight deadlines that information requests come with.

This chapter is not intended as a comprehensive review of IRM practice but to offer a brief guide based on the requirements of the legislation for those who need a refresher on the legal requirements, or for Freedom of Information Officers and DPOs who are coming to this subject new. As such, the international standard for records management (ISO15489) is not covered, although it is worth looking at if you are developing a records management programme.

Information and records management: is it necessary?

The short answer to this question is yes. Data protection, Freedom of Information (FoI) and environmental information all rely on having good records that can be used to support provision of the information requested. If your organization does not have well organized records, it will be difficult to find, identify and provide the information requested, and also to know what information you have provided on request.

The new requirements for record keeping in the GDPR also support the need for good information and records management. Your organization will need to keep track of where personal data is held and what conditions for processing you are using, amongst other tasks. If you cannot provide records to the ICO or the data subject promptly, there will be consequences, up to the imposition of fines. The ICO already has powers to require that information is provided to it by a public authority[1] and can apply to the courts to have the powers of entry and inspection granted if an information notice is not complied with.[2] If your organization cannot comply with an information request due to the state of your information and records management or lack thereof, the reputational damage from an inspection could be severe.

The current Information Commissioner is Elizabeth Durham, who has come from an archives and records management background in British Columbia. Her address to the Archives and Records Association (UK) Annual Conference on 31 August 2017 set out her background and position with regard to records management. In that address[3] she talked of a duty to document that the province of British Columbia in Canada has implemented through an amendment to its Information Management Act. The Information Management Act lays out what government information is, which covers:

> information that:
> - Must be held by law;
> - Documents a decision respecting a course of action that directly affects a person or the operations of a government body;
> - Documents or supports a government body's organization, policies, procedures, transactions or operations;
> - Has archival value; or
> - Relates to matters of court administration assigned to the Attorney General or government by law.[4]

Court records are also covered in a more limited fashion.

The Information Management (Documenting Government Decisions) Amendment Act adds a section on (the Canadian equivalent of the Information Commissioner) the chief records officer's powers that includes the ability to issue directives and guidelines relating to 'the creation of records respecting government information … including, without limitation directives and guidelines respecting the types of records that constitute an adequate record of a government body's decisions'. In other words, if, in the opinion of the chief records officer, a government body should produce specific records in relation to a specific public task, it will be required to. At the time of writing it is not obvious if the amendments have yet actually been made to the Information Management Act or if the chief records officer has used the powers made available to him.

In the UK the courts have not shown a willingness to support a duty to document without direct legislation.

> An Upper Tribunal case involving section 12 of the FoIA[5] stated plainly that FoIA 'is not a statute that prescribes a particular organizational structure or record-keeping practice in public authorities'. In other words, there is no legal requirement to create records or organize them in any particular way just because that would make it easier to answer FoI requests.

To a degree, however, this is not entirely true. There is a Code of Practice on Records Management required by section 46 of the FoIA, which sets out the general principles for managing records in order to support the right to information. Central and local government plus some other public sector bodies are subject to the Public Records Act, which covers the transfer of historical records to a place of deposit like The National Archives (TNA). Any public authorities covered by Crown Copyright have also been required to create an IAR.[6] The GDPR Article 30 record-keeping requirements create a need for other public authorities and private companies to create an IAR for personal data.

Also, from an organizational view, good IRM practice supports staff in their daily work. It should make finding information easier, stop the need to recreate information and clear out old information that will otherwise clog up search results. IRM is the only part of the information governance family that focuses on what information should be retained and what can be disposed of. Information and records destroyed via a retention schedule will not be the cause of fines under the penalties available for tampering and destruction of records in FoI.

So, what is required for good IRM?

The section 46 FoIA/section 61 FoISA Code of Practice for Records Management

The section 46 Code of Practice for Records Management was originally published by the Lord Chancellor, but now published by the ICO, the Code of Practice is clear that it is intended as guidance only, and so is not legally binding, but emphasises that it will help with complying with FoI and the EIR. The section 61 code of practice was produced by the Scottish Ministers.

Both Codes are in two parts. Part 1 covers records management and will apply to all public authorities. Part 2 covers review and transfer of public records and will apply to public authorities that are subject to the relevant Public Records Act. Even if your organization is not subject to a Public Records Act, you may have an archive to transfer records to, so Part 2 will still be helpful in determining arrangements for access for FoI and EIR requests. If you are subject to DPA, you will still have to manage at least personal data records in order to keep to the Article 30 requirements for record keeping, which the Code of Practice will support.

Paragraph 17 of the section 46 Code defines records as 'Information created, received and maintained as evidence and information by an organization or person, in pursuance of legal obligations or in the transaction of business', while paragraph 18 makes it clear that both paper and electronic records are covered.

Part 1: records management

The main principles of records management are as follows:

- Keep records that are necessary to show that an action or a decision was made.
- Keep records only as long as you need to keep them.

- Keep records accessible to those who need to see them.
- Keep records secure from people who do not need to see them.
- Keep records in a manner that means you can rely on them.

The Code of Practice emphasises the necessity of systems and organizational arrangements to manage records correctly. This includes: a records management policy which sets out staff responsibilities towards records; staff training; determining the best methods for storage and access to records; and the creation of disposal/retention schedules. The latter are discussed in further detail below.

The section 61 FoISA code of practice requires an agreed plan on records management to be maintained for Scottish public authorities.

Part 2: Transferring records to archives

The Code of Practice sets out in a very basic manner how and when records should be transferred to archives, for public bodies covered by the Public Records Act 1958, the Public Records (Scotland) Acts 1937 and 2011 and the Public Records (Northern Ireland) Act 1923. The meat of how to transfer them is on the TNA website, which is currently at the following link: http://www.nationalarchives.gov.uk/information-management/manage-information/selection-and-transfer/.[7]

Archival appraisal is outside the scope of this book, but this guidance covers appraising records, selecting records, conducting sensitivity reviews, cataloguing, transferring records and determining access arrangements after transfer. If you do not have to transfer records to TNA, this guidance will still help if you transfer records to another place of deposit or your own organizational archive.

Disposal/retention schedules

Disposal/retention schedules are lists of records, how long they should be kept and what that retention period is based on. Retention periods should include when records should be kept permanently. Staff should be discouraged from using this too liberally – most records do not have historical purposes and can be destroyed in line with the Limitations Act, which is seven years after the last action. There should also be a retention trigger, e.g. seven years after the staff member leaves the organization. You can also include whether records should be destroyed or whether a further review date should be set instead. Depending on your organization's needs, you may also want to include different retention periods for the original or record copy of information and any duplicate copies. It is worth separating out a list of more ephemeral or transitory records like meeting requests that can be deleted very quickly.

Retention schedules can be very detailed, with a line for each type of record, or they can take a 'big bucket approach' or be somewhere in between. 'Big bucket' is an approach in records retention where, instead of identifying all different types of records and giving each type a retention, you group records together in 'buckets' which all get the same retention period; for example, seven years for financial records, general correspondence and anything you could be sued for, which makes seven years the bucket. It will depend on whether the retention schedule is intended more for a computer to use automatically (be very careful with the triggers), for records staff only or for staff use more generally. You will need to balance the audience with the amount of detail that they can handle in order to dispose of records properly, so big bucket may be better for a retention schedule to be used by non-records staff, while a more detailed schedule will work better for professional records staff.

It was relatively easy in the past to manage paper records via a retention schedule. Paper records of a certain age would go into secondary storage, either on- or off-site, and then be destroyed when the records manager said they should be. It is harder to manage the disposal of electronic records. Either they are in structured databases which never get purged, or you have a jumble of shared drives, e-mail systems and other unstructured places that require a lot of manual work to set up for destruction. You may be lucky enough to have an electronic document and records management system which can automatically destroy records, but these do not always include all the records that they should. Some organizations/individual teams have annual clear-out days, which you can encourage with prizes, making sure that electronic records are included.

Information asset registers

As discussed above, these started as a task for public authorities covered by Crown Copyright, to ensure that the general public could get an idea of the information they held. This means that those public authorities are in a good position regarding the GDPR Article 30 record-keeping requirements, as they already have the basic set-up to record where personal data is stored and what the lawful basis is, etc. It also means that other public authorities and private organizations already have a model to follow.

Developing an IAR is a slow process. If you are developing one due to the Article 30 requirements of the GDPR, you can narrow the scope to personal data only.

There are some basics that need to be included – for example, the asset name, how long it should be kept, where it is, who the asset owner is, etc. However, you can include information that suits your organization as well, such as if the information is published and if there are licences related to the data.

Developing the metadata and the template can be the easy part. The harder part is getting the data out of other staff. You can use interviews, provide guidance on how to fill out the template, or a variation of both. Working in focus groups with smaller teams can also work. Bring in the team to go through the template and fill it out with them.

TNA suggests that the IAR is reviewed on a yearly basis. Whatever time period your organization decides on, it makes it clear that a renewal process is required and that you have to keep the IAR up to date for it to be a useful document.

Fitting in records management around other tasks

No book can provide you with more time to do all the tasks that you need to do in one day. However, it can be easy to end up focused on the information rights tasks because they come with deadlines, making records management the bottom of the priority list.

There are a couple of ways to ensure that this does not happen. One is to manage your time as well as possible so that you can ensure that records management is included in your daily and weekly tasks. For example, the last Friday of the month is always the day that the disposal reviews are done, or every August is when the transfer to the archives occurs. Another way is to try to cover two or more things at once. For example, data protection training is likely to include a reference to principle 5, keep no longer than necessary, which would easily link to a reference to the retention schedule and how to use it. Data protection has already been a driver for IARs, and so improving your organization's ability to track its records. Where possible, do records management by preparing for information rights.

Conclusion

Now that you have finished this chapter, you should know:

- why you need to conduct a records management programme;
- what the section 46 code of practice says about managing records;
- what should be in a disposal/retention schedule;
- some tips for fitting in records management with other tasks.

10
Resources

Introduction

You cannot do the jobs of Data Protection and Freedom of Information Officer without outside help. You'll need to pay attention to the guidance produced by the Information Commissioner's Office (ICO) and Scottish Information Commissioner (SIC). Even if you are not subject to the SIC, it is worth keeping an eye on its decisions, as the ICO will be doing so. If you have not already done so, you also need to read the legislation itself. I also recommend reading the decision notices relating to exemptions and exceptions that you are planning to use.

Legislation

The UK Freedom of Information Act (FoIA), 1998 and 2018 Data Protection Acts (DPAs), Environmental Information Regulations (EIR) and all the other Regulations are available through the legislation.gov.uk website. The Scottish legislation is available there as well. A web search on any of this legislation should bring up the direct link to it on this website.

The General Data Protection Regulation (GDPR) and other EU legislation are also available on the EUR-Lex.europa.eu website, but only as a hard-to-navigate HTML site or PDF. A better link to the GDPR is available here: https://gdpr-info.eu/.[1] This separates out the

Articles and Recitals as separate links, grouped by theme and Chapter, and makes the document so much easier to navigate.

You can also find the debates in the Houses of Lords and Commons relating to the 2018 DPA on the UK Parliament website. The 2018 DPA does not contain the text of the GDPR, so you will need access to both.

Guidance

For UK guidance on Data Protection, FoI and the EIR, go to the ICO's website: www.ico.org.uk. The guidance is split between what the public need to know and what organizations need to know. The ICO also has a helpline, including one specifically for small organizations, although I have tended to find that this is not very helpful if you have a question relating to something for which there is no case law.

For Scottish organizations, this type of guidance is available from the SIC website: www.itspublicknowledge.info/home/ScottishInformationCommissioner.aspx. Although the advice is specific to Scottish legislation, it is worth checking out if you are using a similar exemption/exception in UK law to see if the argument you are making has been rejected by the SIC. The SIC guidance on managing voice recordings for requests could also help to manage verbally made Environmental Information requests.

For data protection purposes, you will also need to take into account the Article 29 Working Party guidance, which is available at the following link: http://ec.europa.eu/newsroom/article29/news.cfm?item_type=1360.

Legal cases

Keeping an eye on the case law in information rights is important. If you do not keep up to date with decisions and case law relating to exemptions you may try to use an argument that has already been rejected. While you should take into account ICO and SIC decisions, these are not case law. This means that their decisions do not create precedent. The Information Tribunal and higher courts of England, Wales and Scotland do create precedent, so if they say that an exemption should be interpreted in a particular way, you need to act accordingly.

Both the ICO and the SIC keep a list of the decisions they have made on their websites.

The next tier in the UK is the Information Tribunal, whose decisions can be found at the following link: http://informationrights.decisions.tribunals.gov.uk/Public/search.aspx. This is the point at which case law is formed, so remember that any Information Tribunal decisions are required to be followed, unless a higher court says otherwise.

Higher court cases can be found via BAILLI, which covers UK, Scottish and Irish cases, with other British Isles jurisdictions as well. This can be accessed at the following link: www.bailii.org/. Where there is a legal report in a higher court, it should be available here. But how do you find out about these cases?

Social media, blogs and listservs

There are many people 'out there' on social media in this area, and there are some that I find it useful to follow. Twitter in particular is my news service for information rights. I follow the ICO and SIC Twitter accounts, and also:

- @FoIManUK, who also has a useful blog;
- @tim2040, who also has a useful blog. Generally stronger on data protection-related issues;
- @tpittpayne, a barrister at 11KBW who represents FoI and data protection cases at the Information Tribunal and other courts;
- @cbridgeinfo, covers data protection from an Irish perspective.

Start following a few people, and you'll find others whom you want to follow.

A very useful blog for Information Rights law in the UK is Panopticon, run by 11KBW. The blog focuses on cases that these lawyers represent at the Information Tribunal and higher courts.

You should also join listservs or e-mail groups that swap information on information rights law. This will help you to identify when a round robin request has been received and to swap policies and procedures with people working in the same area as you.

Notes

Chapter 1

1 www.freedominfo.org/2016/12/eight-countries-adopt-foi-regimes-2016/ [accessed 5 January 2017].
2 https://www.foia.gov/faq.html#exemptions [accessed 16 May 2017].
3 The EEA includes all EU members, Norway, Iceland and Liechtenstein.
4 [2003] EWCA Civ 1746, para 28.
5 [2014] EWCA Civ 92, which will be discussed further in Chapter 4.
6 Eight data protection principles in the DPA have become six in the GDPR, as data subject rights and transfers outside the EU have become their own articles.
7 S 40 in the UK FoIA and s 38 in the FoISA.

Chapter 2

1 Freedom of Information Act 2000, c.36.
2 Freedom of Information (Scotland) Act 2002, asp 13.
3 Freedom of Information Act 2000, c.36, s 1(3), Freedom of Information (Scotland) Act 2002, asp 13, s 1(3).
4 Freedom of Information Act 2000, c.36, s 1(4), Freedom of Information (Scotland) Act 2002, asp 13, s 1(4).
5 Freedom of Information Act 2000, c.36.
6 Freedom of Information (Scotland) Act 2002, asp 13, s 8(1)(a).
7 Scottish Information Commissioner, 'Guidance on Information

Requests, Telephone Calls and Voicemail: Are verbal requests valid?'
8 Scottish Information Commissioner Decision 061/2014, para 11.
9 Information Commissioner Decision Notice FS50523573.
10 Information Commissioner's Office, 'Consideration of identity of motives of the applicant', pp. 4–5, para 15.
11 Information Commissioner Decision Notice FS50611991, para 10.
12 [2015] UKIT EA/2015/0140.
13 [2015] UKIT EA/2015/0140, para 27.
14 *Ibid.*
15 *Ibid.*
16 *Ibid.*, para 28.
17 *Ibid.*, para 29.
18 *Ibid.*
19 S 1(3) for both Acts.
20 Information Commissioner Decision Notices FS50596075 and FS50437321.
21 Information Commissioner Decision Notice FS50589287.
22 Information Commissioner Decision Notice FS50596075, para 37.
23 *Ibid.*, para 38.
24 Information Commissioner Decision Notice FS50611176.
25 Scottish Information Commissioner Decision 073/2015, para 31.
26 Information Commissioner Decision Notices FS50455014, FS50465008; Scottish Information Commissioner Decisions 207/2012 and 060/2013.
27 Information Commissioner Decision Notice FS50465008, para 33.
28 Information Commissioner's Office, 'Recognising a request made under the Freedom of Information Act Section 8 v1.2', para 110, p. 20.
29 Joint Information Systems Committee, usually known by its acronym. An organization funded by universities in the UK to look into information technology, management and legal issues.
30 Available here: https://www.jisc.ac.uk/guides/managing-information/how-long [accessed 27 January 2017].
31 One example can be found here: www.datix.co.uk/products-services/modules/uk-and-europe/freedom-of-information/ [accessed 27 January 2017].
32 In Higher Education, JISC carries out a yearly survey on information rights requests which sets out the categories for the sector to use.
33 Freedom of Information Act 2000, c.36, s 10(1).
34 *Ibid.*, s 10(6).

35 Freedom of Information (Scotland) Act 2002, asp 13, s 10(1)(b).
36 *Ibid.*, Section 73.
37 Information Commissioner's Office, 'Time for Compliance', para 32.
38 [2007] UKIT EA/2006/0049, paragraph 63.
39 Freedom of Information (Fees for Required Disclosure) (Scotland) Regulations 2004 No. 467 Regulation 5.
40 Freedom of Information Act 2000, c.36, s 1(3).
41 *Ibid.*, Section 16.
42 The Freedom of Information and Data Protection (Appropriate Limit and Fees) Regulations 2004 No. 3244, Regulation 7(4).
43 Freedom of Information Act 2000, c.36, s 17(7).

Chapter 3

1 Freedom of Information Act 2000, c.36, s 2(1).
2 Freedom of Information (Scotland) Act 2002, asp 13, ss.28–35, 39(1) or 41.
3 www.law-democracy.org/wp-content/uploads/2012/05/Yemen.FOI_.Apr12.V2.pdf [accessed 5 January 2017].
4 The Freedom of Information and Data Protection (Appropriate Limit and Fees) Regulation 2004 SI 2004 No. 3244 and The Freedom of Information (Fees for Required Disclosure) (Scotland) Regulations 2004 No. 467.
5 The Freedom of Information and Data Protection (Appropriate Limit and Fees) Regulations 2004, No. 3244, Regulation 6(3)(c).
6 Information Commissioner's Office, 'Information readily accessible to the applicant by other means (Section 21)', para 31.
7 Access to Health Records Act 1990 c.23.
8 Antisocial Behaviour Etc. (Scotland) Act 2004 asp 8.
9 [2012] UKIT EA/2012/0229, para 13.
10 Freedom of Information Act 2000, c.36, s 22A(1); Freedom of Information (Scotland) Act 2002, asp 13, s 27(2).
11 Information Commissioner's Office, 'Information intended for future publication and research information (sections 22 and 22A)', para 44.
12 *Ibid.*, para 45.
13 Scottish Information Commissioner, 'Section 27: Information intended for future publication: Exemption Briefing', para 26.

14 Information Commissioner's Office, 'Information intended for future publication and research information (sections 22 and 22A)', para 46.
15 Scottish Information Commissioner, 'Section 27: Information intended for future publication: Exemption Briefing', para 27.
16 Information Commissioner's Office, 'Security bodies (section 23)', para 24 and Scottish Information Commissioner, 'Section 31 Exemption Briefing', para 7.
17 Information Commissioner's Office, 'Security bodies (section 23)', example from para 20.
18 Information Commissioner's Office, 'Freedom of Information Act Awareness Guidance No. 14 International Relations', p. 3–4.
19 Information Commissioner Decision Notice FS50611149.
20 Information Commissioner's Office, 'The economy (section 29)', para 5.
21 *Ibid.*, para 7.
22 *Ibid.*, para 10.
23 Scottish Information Commissioner, 'Section 34: Investigations by Scottish public authorities and proceedings arising out of such investigations: Exemption Briefing'.
24 Information Commissioner's Office, 'Law enforcement (section 31)', para 33.
25 *Ibid.*, para 44.
26 Information Commissioner's Office, 'Government policy (section 35)', para 134.
27 *Ibid.*, para 140.
28 S 40(1) of the FoIA and s 38(1)(a) of the FoISA exempt personal data of the data subject.
29 Freedom of Information Act 2000, c.36, s 40(2)(b), 40(3)(a)(i) and 40(3)(b).
30 Freedom of Information Act 2000, c.36, s 40(3)(a)(ii).
31 *Ibid.*, s 40(4).
32 Freedom of Information (Scotland) Act 2002, asp 13, s 38(1)(c).
33 *Ibid.*, s 38(1)(d).
34 [1968] F.S.R.415 *Coco v AN Clark (Engineers) Ltd.*
35 Information Commissioner's Office, 'Prohibitions on disclosure (section 44)', para 12 example.
36 2012 UKUT 440 AAC, para 28.
37 https://www.whatdotheyknow.com/.

Chapter 4

1 General Data Protection Regulation (EU) 2016/679, Article 32(1)(d).
2 Article 29 Working Party, 'Guidelines on Personal data breach notification under Regulation 2016/679', p. 9.
3 General Data Protection Regulation (EU) 2016/679, Article 6(b).
4 https://ico.org.uk/for-organizations/guide-to-data-protection/conditions-for-processing/ [accessed 1 August 2017].
5 Data Protection Act 1998 c.29, Schedule 2, s 5(d).
6 General Data Protection Regulation (EU) 2016/679, Article 6(f).
7 General Data Protection Regulation (EU) 2016/679, Recital 54.
8 General Data Protection Regulation (EU) 2016/679, Recital 56.
9 General Data Protection Regulation (EU) 2016/679, Article 4(7).
10 General Data Protection Regulation (EU) 2016/679, Article 4(8).
11 General Data Protection Regulation (EU) 2016/679, Article 82(2).
12 General Data Protection Regulation (EU) 2016/679, Article 25.
13 The Data Protection (Charges and Information) Regulations 2018, Regulation 3(1).
14 https://ico.org.uk/media/for-organizations/documents/2172937/gdpr-documentation-controller-template.xlsx [accessed 29 March 2018].

Chapter 5

1 *Halsbury's Laws of England*, volume 37, 3rd edition.
2 GDPR, Article 15(3).
3 GDPR, Article 15(1).
4 GDPR, Article 4(1).
5 GDPR, Article 12(6).
6 *Durant v Financial Services Authority*, [2003] EWCA Civ 1746.
7 *Ibid.*, paragraph 28.
8 GDPR, Article 12(5).
9 *Ibid.*
10 GDPR, Recital 15.
11 GDPR, Article 12(1).
12 *Ibid.*
13 GDPR, Article 12(3).
14 GDPR, Article 23.
15 https://ico.org.uk/for-organizations/guide-to-data-protection/exemptions/ [accessed 5 September 2017].

16 GDPR, Article 17(1).
17 GDPR, Article 18(2).
18 GDPR, Article 18(1).
19 GDPR, Article 21.
20 Article 29 Data Protection Working Party, 'Guidance on the right to data portability', WP 242 rev.01, p. 12.
21 GDPR, Article 22(1).
22 GDPR, Article 4(4).
23 GDPR, Article 22(3).

Chapter 6

1 See the section on 'The right to be informed in practice', https://ico.org.uk/for-organizations/guide-to-the-general-data-protection-regulation-gdpr/individual-rights/right-to-be-informed/ [accessed 9 September 2018].
2 Article 29 Working Party, 'Guidelines on Data Protection Impact Assessment (DPIA) and determining whether processing is "likely to result in a high risk" for the purposes of Regulation 2016/679', p. 9.
3 General Data Protection Regulation (EU) 2016/679, Article 44.
4 General Data Protection Regulation (EU) 2016/679, Article 46(2).
5 General Data Protection Regulation (EU) 2016/679, Article 47(1).
6 General Data Protection Regulation (EU) 2016/679, Article 49(1).
7 The Protection of Freedoms Act 2012 c.9.

Chapter 7

1 UN/ECE Convention on Access to Information, Public Participation in Decision-Making and Access to Justice in Environmental Matters.
2 The Directive is Directive 2003/4/EC, Public Access to Environmental Information.
3 Information Commissioner's Office, 'What is Environmental Information (Regulation 2(1) EIR)', p. 9.
4 *Ibid.*
5 *Ibid.*
6 *Ibid.*, p. 10.
7 [2009] UKIT EA/2009/0001, 24 June 2009.
8 *Ibid.*, p. 29.

9 [2008] UKIT EA/2007/0072.
10 *Ibid.*, para 65.
11 Environmental Information Regulations 2004 No. 3391, Regulation 3 and Environmental Information Regulations (Scotland) 2004 No. 520, Regulation 3.
12 Environmental Information Regulations 2004 No. 3391, Regulation 2(2) and Environmental Information Regulations (Scotland) 2004 No. 520, Regulation 2(1).
13 [2015] UKUT 0052 (AAC). Paragraph 7 under Section C.
14 *Ibid.*, para 126.
15 Information Commissioner Decision Notice FER0534921.
16 Information Commissioner's Office, 'Public Authorities under the EIR Environmental Information Regulations', para 28.
17 Scottish Information Commissioner Decision Notice 118/2014, para 29.
18 *Ibid.*, para 34.
19 Environmental Information Regulations 2004 No. 3391, Regulation 7(1). The Scottish Regulations use slightly different language to make the same point.
20 Environmental Information Regulations 2004 No. 3391, Regulation 10 and Environmental Information Regulations (Scotland) 2004 No. 520, Regulation 3.
21 Code of Practice on the discharge of the obligations of public authorities under the Environmental Information Regulations 2004 (SI 2004 No. 3391) Issued under Regulation 16 of the Regulations, February 2005, para 34.
22 Environmental Information Regulations 2004 No. 3391, Regulation 8 and Environmental Information Regulations (Scotland) 2004 No. 520, Regulation 8.
23 CJEU C-71/14.
24 *Ibid.*, para 45.
25 Accessed 14 March 2017.
26 Environment Information Regulations 2004 No. 3391, Regulation 12(4). Regulation 10(4) in the Scottish Regulations refers to Scottish public authorities rather than 'a public authority'.
27 Information Commissioner's Office, 'Manifestly unreasonable requests regulation 12(4)(b): Environmental Information Regulations', para 16.
28 [2012] UKUT 442 (AAC).
29 C-233/00 [2003] ECR I-6625, *Commission v France*.

30 [2012] UKUT 442 (AAC), para 44 .
31 [2012] UKUT 440 (AAC), *Dransfield v Information Commissioner*.
32 Information Commissioner's Office, 'Manifestly unreasonable requests regulation 12(4)(b): Environmental Information Regulations', para 20.
33 Information Commissioner Decision Notice FS50464000.
34 [2008] UKIT EA/2008/0052.
35 Scottish Information Commissioner Decision Notice 044/2009.
36 Environmental Information Regulations 2004 No. 3391, Regulation 12(8).
37 Information Commissioner Decision Notice FER0184525.
38 [2009] UKIT EA/2008/0052.
39 Environmental Information Regulations 2004 No. 3391, Regulation 12(5) and Environmental Information Regulations (Scotland) 2004 No. 520, Regulation 10(5).
40 [2007] UKIT EA/2006/0037.
41 Information Commissioner Decision Notice FER0282488.
42 Information Commissioner's Office, 'International relations, defence, national security or public safety (regulation 12(5)(a)): Environmental Information Regulations', p. 13.
43 [2006] UKIT EA/2006/0078.
44 [2007] UKIT EA/2007/0022.
45 Information Commissioner's Office, 'The course of justice and inquiries exception (regulation 12(5)(b)): Environmental Information Regulations', p. 7.
46 Information Commissioner's Office, 'Intellectual property rights (regulation 12(5)(c)): Environmental Information Regulations', p. 3.
47 Copyright, Designs and Patents Act 1988 c.48, s 50.
48 This was covered in [2012] UKUT 491 ACC.
49 [2010] UKIT EA/2010/0012.
50 Information Commissioner's Office, 'Confidentiality of commercial or industrial information (regulation 12(5)(e)): Environmental Information Regulations', para 38. Examples of illegitimate interests are also provided in paragraph 41.
51 Environmental Information Regulations 2004 No. 3391, Regulation 13(1) and Environmental Information Regulations (Scotland) 2004 No. 520, Regulation 11(1).

Chapter 8

1 Access to Health Records Act 1990 c.23.
2 Data Protection Act 1998 c.29, s 69.
3 Access to Medical Reports Act 1988 c.28.
4 Care Act 2014 c.23, s 122(3).
5 Local Government (Access to Information) Act 1985 c.43.
6 Re-use of Public Sector Information Regulations 2015 No. 1415.
7 *Ibid.*, Regulation 6(d).
8 https://www.nationalarchives.gov.uk/information-management/re-using-public-sector-information/uk-government-licensing-framework/open-government-licence/copyright-notices-attribution-statements/ [accessed 29 March 2018].
9 Re-use of Public Sector Information Regulations 2015 No. 1415, Regulation 15(10).
10 Information Commissioner Decision Notice FS50619465.
11 *Ibid.*, para 23.
12 The Privacy and Electronic Communications (EC Directive) Regulations 2003 No. 2426.
13 https://ico.org.uk/for-organizations/guide-to-pecr/key-concepts-and-definitions/ [accessed 29 March 2018].
14 www.tpsonline.org.uk/tps/index.html [accessed 29 March 2018].
15 Computer Misuse Act 1990 c.18.
16 https://www.nationalarchives.gov.uk/documents/foi-section-46-code-of-practice.pdf [accessed 29 March 2018].
17 Public Records Act 1958 c.51 (Regnal. 6_and_7_Eliz_2).
18 The INSPIRE Regulations 2009 No. 3157.

Chapter 9

1 Freedom of Information Act, s 51.
2 *Ibid.*, Schedule 3.
3 https://ico.org.uk/about-the-ico/news-and-events/news-and-blogs/2017/08/archives-and-records-association-annual-conference/ [accessed 25 September 2017].
4 British Columbia Corporate Information and Records Management Office, 'A Practitioner's Guide to the Information Management Act: Frequently Asked Questions about the Act', pp. 1–2.
5 [2014] UKUT 479 (AAC), para 42.

6 OPSI, 'Future management of Crown Copyright', Chapter 8.

7 Accessed 28 September 2017. This link is more direct than the link in the Code of Practice.

Chapter 10

1 Accessed 29 March 2018.

Index

HBD adhya-4963 16/6/22 RTK